First published in the United Kingdom in 2018 by
Pavilion
43 Great Ormond Street
London WC1N 3HZ

ISBN 978-1-91162-441-7

A CIP catalogue record for this book is available from the
British Library

10 9 8 7 6 5 4 3 2 1

Reproduction by Mission, Hong Kong
Printed and bound by 1010 Printing International Ltd, China

This book can be ordered direct from the publisher at
www.pavilionbooks.com

Neither the author nor the publisher can accept responsibility
for any injury or illness that may arise as a result of following the
advice contained in this work. Any application of the information
contained in the book is at the reader's sole discretion.

MOB
VEGGIE

BEN LEBUS

PAVILION

INTRODUCING... 6

BRUNCH MOB 8

FRESH MOB 30

SPEEDY MOB 52

INTRODUCING...

What's up Veggie MOB! Welcome to the second MOB Kitchen book, jammed full of the most delicious vegetarian meals you'll ever munch. All for under a tenner. All using the freshest ingredients. Same old MOB, veggie-style.

Producing a solely veggie book has been a dream of mine since I started MOB Kitchen. As the MOB has grown, there has been an undeniable enthusiasm surrounding our vegetarian dishes, and it is clear that the people are taking up increasingly meat-free diets. I am a firm believer in vegetarian dishes being as tasty if not tastier than many meat dishes – the thousands of veggie MOB recipe recreations that you send to us really shows this.

MOB Kitchen is committed to being sustainable. The food industry has come under a lot of scrutiny regarding waste and climate change, and we want the *MOB Veggie* cookbook to help promote a change in people's eating habits, whether they are vegetarian or not. At MOB Kitchen, we are determined to do our bit for the environment and with this book, we hope you will be able to as well. With meat-based agriculture accounting for 14.5% of greenhouse gases, it is essential that we cut our meat intake because this is the most significant way in which you can do your bit in preventing climate change. So why not help save our planet while eating delicious food?

While planning and testing the recipes for this book, I realized how easy it is to take up a vegetarian or vegan diet simply by making some clever food swaps. For example, switching your honey for maple syrup or agave. Your butter for veggie margarine. Yogurt for coconut yogurt. Milk for oat milk. And so on. The meat-free products industry is evolving and expanding so rapidly, and so making these switches is both easy and affordable.

With still nearly 800 battery farms in the UK and a continued need to cut out down on meat intake, it is time to change the status quo for veggie dishes. People need to be enthusiastic about vegetarian recipes and start to move away from a predominantly meat-based diet. And with that in mind, this book contains both vegetarian and vegan dishes that are as good, if not better, than their meat-based counterparts. We have introduced the wonderful meaty jackfruit that can be bought in a can and makes the Mighty Jackfruit Curry feel so rich you wouldn't even know that it's vegan. Discovering this fruit has opened my eyes to world of simple, 'meaty textured' vegan dishes and there's no looking back! Tofu can be equally as 'meaty' and our Black Pepper Tofu is insanely good. There is also our Big Boy Bhaji Burgers, a classic from the MOB – not the predictable bean burger that appears on burger menus as the vegetarian option – this beast goes down an absolute treat.

We've got all of your favourite chapters from the first MOB book, filled with the most delicious veggie and vegan recipes. As with the first book, all we assume you have is salt, pepper and olive oil. With MOB Classics such as butternut squash pancakes, quick peri peri halloumi burgers and spinach and ricotta cannelloni, this book has it all. Every single recipe comes with a Spotify code, so start scanning, blast the tunes and get cooking. So that music is at the heart of the experience in each recipe! As with the first book, every single recipe feeds four people for very little money, busting the myth that delicious veggie dishes come at a higher price.

The book is split into six chapters, starting with Brunch MOB, which brings fresh, unique recipes to the breakfast game. You'll no longer have to pay extra for your veggie fry up at the fancy cafe. Second up is Fresh MOB, full of simple salads, soups and some banging veggie feasts bursting with flavour. Numero three is Speedy MOB. All the recipes take 30 minutes or less, no skill is needed and they're perfect for lunches or quick suppers. Next we have Fuss-free MOB. At uni it was such a pain washing up loads of dishes after a big dinner, so ALL of these recipes are one-dish wonders. Easy as 1, 2, 3. The fifth chapter is Flashy MOB. These recipes are a bit more involved, great for a weekend dinner party. So get your MOB over and show them your skills. The final chapter is Fakeaway MOB, featuring recipes for fast food, veggie-style, but you can actually do them at home. AND, they are fresher, cheaper, healthier and much more delicious!

MOB Veggie is the ultimate veggie cookbook, with everything you need to make the perfect vegetarian dishes. Never again will you struggle to cater for your vegan or Veggie MOB – this book has it all.

Big love, Ben

KEY TO SYMBOLS
[★] MOB classic (one of the best-loved recipes from the channel)
[VG] Vegan

When you see one of the following Spotify Codes, you can scan it using the Spotify app to listen to the corresponding playlist/song.

Open 🟢 | Search 🔍 | Scan 📷

1

BRUNCH
MOB

INGREDIENTS

6 fresh beetroots (beets)
10 eggs
soy sauce
sesame oil
fresh ginger
fresh coriander (cilantro)
crushed chillies
2 avocados
1 lime
olive oil
salt and pepper

**THE BEST RÖSTI YOU'LL
EVER EAT. KEEP THEM IN
THE OVEN UNTIL THEY ARE
CRISPY. TRUST US, THEY'LL
GET THERE AND IT'S WELL
WORTH THE WAIT.**

CRISPY ASIAN BEETROOT RÖSTIS [★]

01 Preheat your oven to 180°C fan (200°C/400°F/Gas Mark 6).

02 Coarsely grate the fresh beetroots. Squeeze out the gratings to remove excess moisture. Add to a bowl with 2 eggs and whisk with a fork.

03 Add 2 tablespoons of soy sauce and 1½ teaspoons of sesame oil. Add 2 teaspoons of grated ginger, a handful of chopped coriander and a teaspoon of crushed chillies. Mix everything together well.

04 Lay some baking paper on a baking tray.

05 Divide the rösti mix into 8 patties. Lay them on the baking tray. Place in the preheated oven for 45 minutes, turning them after 30 minutes.

06 Guac time. Mash the avocados in a bowl. Add the juice of a lime and a small handful of chopped coriander. Add a drizzle of olive oil, and season with salt and pepper. Cover and chill.

07 Egg time. Boil a pan of water. Carefully crack each egg (you'll need 4) into a glass. With a fork or a whisk, create a little whirlpool in the water. Pour the egg into the water, not in the centre of the whirlpool, but on the edge. The water will fold the white over the yolk and should form a nice little ball. Repeat for the other eggs.

08 Cook each egg for 3 minutes over a medium heat. To check if it's done, just gently lift the egg with a spoon. If the white is still a bit wobbly, leave it for 10 more seconds. If it's firm, remove from the heat.

09 Remove the röstis from the oven – they should be nice and crispy at this point.

10 Serve the röstis with a big dollop of guac, with the poached egg resting on top. Add a drop or two of sesame oil and then dig in!

CHICKPEA SHAKSHUKA

SERVES 4
45 mins

Nérija
Valleys

INGREDIENTS

2 onions
2 red (bell) peppers
garlic
fresh coriander (cilantro)
tomato purée (paste)
paprika
ground cumin
hot chilli powder
2 x 400-g (14-oz) tins of
tomatoes
400-g (14-oz) tin of chickpeas
8 eggs
sourdough bread
1 lemon
vegetable oil
salt and pepper

A ONE-DISH WONDER. ZERO-FUSS. ZERO EFFORT. MAKE SURE YOU FRY THOSE SPICES TO ALLOW THEM TO RELEASE THEIR NATURAL OILS AND REACH THEIR FULL POTENTIAL.

01 Dice your onions, peppers and 2 garlic cloves. Finely chop some coriander.

02 Heat a large frying pan (skillet), add a glug of oil and chuck in your diced veg. Sauté for 5 minutes, stirring regularly (or until the veg is softened).

03 Add a tablespoon of tomato purée, some salt and pepper, 1½ teaspoons of paprika, 1½ teaspoons of ground cumin, 1½ teaspoons of chilli powder and a handful of chopped coriander. Fry for 3 minutes, stirring frequently, allowing the spices to release their flavours.

04 Add the tomatoes to the pan.

05 Drain your chickpeas, rinse them, then add them to the pan. Simmer for 10 minutes on low.

06 Add the eggs and put on the lid. Wait until the eggs are cooked through.

07 Toast the sourdough to serve with it, finish with a squeeze of lemon and the remaining chopped coriander.

INGREDIENTS

1 white onion
5 potatoes (ideally with red skins)
10 eggs
120 g (4 oz) pitted green olives
fresh parsley
175-g (6-oz) block of manchego
olive oil
salt and pepper

THE BREAKFAST OF KINGS. THE MANCHEGO MAKES THIS. IT'S EXPENSIVE, BUT WE BUDGETED SO YOU CAN STILL BUY IT AND KEEP THE SHOPPING COST LOW.

SPANISH TORTILLA [★]

01 Slice the white onion into discs. Halve the discs, and then add to a frying pan (skillet). Fry until soft and slightly browned, and then remove from the pan and set aside.

02 Slice the potatoes into discs. Add them to the pan, and fry until soft, and browned on each side (roughly 5 minutes each side over a medium heat). Remove from the heat and set aside.

03 Into a big bowl, crack the eggs. Chop the green olives and add them to the bowl with a handful of chopped parsley (save some for garnish), your cooked onions and potatoes, and a good sprinkle of salt and pepper. Whisk everything together. This is your tortilla mix.

04 Pour some oil into a large pan and place over a medium–low heat. Pour the tortilla mix into the pan. Crumble ¾ of the manchego on top. Cook for 15 minutes, occasionally running a spatula around the edge so it doesn't stick.

05 After 15 minutes, remove the pan from the heat, and place a large plate on top of it. In one quick motion, flip the pan over, so the plate is now on the bottom. The tortilla should now be resting on the plate.

06 Place the pan back on the heat. Slide the tortilla off the plate and back into the pan, making sure you push all the bits of potato and onion under the tortilla as you do this.

07 Cook for 5 more minutes on a medium–low heat, then remove the pan. Place the plate back on top, and flip the pan again.

08 Grate over the last of your manchego, and add a small handful of parsley. The perfect breakfast. Enjoy.

CHANGING THE BRUNCH
GAME FOREVER, THESE
PANCAKES ARE THE
BUSINESS. THE SWEET
AND SAVOURY COMBO OF
THE CHEESE AND MAPLE
SYRUP WORKS A TREAT.

BUTTERNUT SQUASH PANCAKES [★]

01 Preheat your oven to 180°C fan (200°C/400°F/Gas Mark 6).

02 Slice the butternut squash into slices and put on a baking tray. Drizzle with olive oil and season with salt and pepper. Roast in the preheated oven for 50 minutes.

03 Once the butternut squash is soft, remove it from the oven. Add it to a mixing bowl and mash it up. Sift in 250 g (2 cups) self-raising flour and mix it all together with a fork. Then add 350 ml (1½ cups) whole milk, bit by bit. It will be a bit lumpy, but don't worry.

04 Crack in the eggs and add 60 g (1 cup) grated Parmesan and 1½ teaspoons of chopped rosemary. Season with salt and pepper and mix together. It should be a nice thick consistency. If needs be, just add a bit more flour.

05 Add some butter to a frying pan (skillet) or pancake pan and allow it to get hot.

06 Add 2 ladles of your pancake batter to the pan. Cook for 3–4 minutes on each side. Repeat with the remaining mixture.

07 Stack up your pancakes, drizzle over some maple syrup, sprinkle on some more Parmesan and get stuck in!

FETA & BLACK BEAN TACOS WITH HOMEMADE GUAC

SERVES 4
45 mins

Yung Bae
Sometime

INGREDIENTS

2 avocados
1 red onion
fresh coriander (cilantro)
2 limes
200-g (7-oz) packet of radishes
1 red chilli
red wine vinegar
400-g (14-oz) tin of black beans

01 Peel and mash the avocados and mix well.

02 Halve, peel and dice the red onion and add half of it to the avocado. Roughly chop half the coriander and add to the mix. Squeeze in the juice of a lime and add salt, pepper and olive oil. Mix well and set the guac aside.

03 Thinly slice your whole radishes and do the same for your red chilli. Add plenty of salt and drizzle with red wine vinegar. Add to the avocado mix but leave a few radishes to garnish.

04 Use a sieve (strainer) to drain the water from your black beans and rinse them under the tap (faucet). Add to a saucepan along with the other half of your red onion over a medium heat with a glug of olive oil.

garlic
paprika
ground cumin
6 eggs
200-g (7-oz) block of feta
small tortilla wraps
olive oil
salt and pepper

**A GREAT DISH FOR A BIG
SHARING BREAKFAST.
THIS IS ONE FOR THE
HANGOVER.**

05 Crush or finely slice 2 garlic cloves and add to the beans along with 1 teaspoon paprika and 1 teaspoon cumin. Cook for 2–3 minutes. Remove from the heat and cover to keep warm.

06 Crack the eggs into a saucepan and whisk to combine. Add a pinch of salt and pepper and crumble half the feta block into the egg mixture.

07 Scramble your eggs and feta over a medium–low heat, stirring and scraping as you go. Be careful not to overcook!

08 Heat your tortillas either in a pan or under the grill (broiler). Just a few minutes will do.

09 Assemble your tacos with a generous scoop of your feta-scrambled eggs, a spoonful of your spiced black beans, the remaining radishes, chilli, feta and coriander. Finish with an extra squeeze of lime and a pinch of salt.

INGREDIENTS

5 red chillies
garlic
fresh ginger
400 g (2¼ cups) basmati rice
(we use Tilda)
4 carrots
2 brown onions
fresh coriander (cilantro)
1 white cabbage
soy sauce
sugar
2 limes
4 eggs
vegetable oil

A CLASSIC INDONESIAN
FRIED RICE DISH. VEGGIE-
FIED. YOU CAN VEGANISE
THIS DISH SIMPLY BY
LEAVING OUT THE FRIED
EGGS. SOMETHING ABOUT
THAT SPICY HIT IN THE
MORNING REALLY GETS
YOU GOING.

VEGGIE NASI GORENG

01 Preheat your oven to 220°C fan (240°C/475°F/Gas Mark 9).

02 Place 4 of the red chillies on a lined baking sheet and bake for 5 minutes.

03 Add 2 unpeeled garlic cloves and a large piece of ginger (unpeeled, too), then continue to bake for around another 20 minutes, or until the garlic cloves turn sticky, the chillies start to go black and the ginger is soft. Turn down the heat to 180°C fan (200°C/400°F/Gas Mark 6) if anything starts to look like it's burning.

04 Meanwhile, put the basmati rice on (cook according to the instructions on the packet) and prep your veggies. Grate your carrots and a small piece of ginger, finely slice the onions, 4 garlic cloves and 1 red chilli, and chop up the coriander stalks. Slice up your cabbage into bite-sized pieces.

05 Back to the sauce. Cut the roasted chilli stalks off, and peel the garlic cloves and ginger. Put these, along with 4 tablespoons of soy sauce, 1 teaspoon of sugar and the juice of a lime into a blender and blend.

06 In a large frying pan (skillet), pour in some oil. Start by frying the onions and garlic on a low heat until softened. Then add the cabbage, the grated ginger and the sliced red chilli. Allow to soften and then add the coriander stalks and the grated carrot.

07 Mix and cook for another 5 minutes, then add your rice and the sauce.

08 Mix it all together and cook until the sauce is fully mixed in.

09 Meanwhile, fry the eggs in a separate non-stick frying pan.

10 Serve the rice steaming hot, with a squeeze of lime, top with an egg, then cut into those runny yolks!

INGREDIENTS

plain (all-purpose) flour

chickpea (gram) flour

4 sweet potatoes

1 red onion

garlic

fresh ginger

2 red chillies

fresh coriander (cilantro)

mustard seeds

fennel seeds

cumin seeds

ground turmeric

1 lime

olive oil

salt and pepper

A DELICIOUS, SPICED
ALTERNATIVE TO
PANCAKES. YOU WANT TO
MASH THE SWEET POTATO
A BIT WHEN IT'S IN THE
PAN TO MAKE IT NICE
AND FLUFFY.

BRUNCH SWEET POTATO DOSAS [VG]

01 Pour 100 g (¾ cup) of each flour into a large bowl with 375 ml (1½ cups) of water, and use a whisk to mix the ingredients into a smooth batter. Cover and place in the fridge for at least an hour. It will keep for up to 5 days.

02 Preheat your oven to 200°C fan (220°C/450°F/Gas Mark 8).

03 Chop your sweet potatoes into cubes and drizzle with olive oil, then season with salt and pepper. Cook for 30 minutes or until the sweet potato is soft and caramelized.

04 Chop the onion, 4 garlic cloves, a 2.5-cm (1-inch) piece of ginger, 1 red chilli (de-seed it first) and the coriander stalks.

05 Add some olive oil to a frying pan (skillet), then fry 2 teaspoons each of mustard seeds, fennel seeds and cumin seeds until they are fragrant.

06 Add your chopped onion, garlic, ginger, chilli and coriander. Fry over a low heat until soft. Add a teaspoon of ground turmeric and the roasted sweet potato. Mix well, semi-mashing the sweet potato.

07 Oil a frying pan, pour a ladle of batter into the pan and move your ladle in a circular motion to create a thin pancake.

08 Flip and cook so that both sides are golden brown and crispy. Repeat with the rest of the mixture.

09 Take a dosa, spoon in some sweet potato filling, and finish with a bit of lime juice, more chopped red chilli and some chopped coriander leaves. Enjoy, MOB!

SERVES 4

40 mins

Tom Misch

Water Baby

INGREDIENTS

1 red onion

garlic

250-g (9-oz) packet of cherry tomatoes

100 g (3½ oz) pitted olives

capers

dried oregano

2 x 200-g (7-oz) blocks of feta

nice ciabatta loaf

fresh parsley

butter

olive oil

salt and pepper

THIS ONE IS PERFECT FOR WHEN YOU HAVE A GROUP OF PEOPLE ROUND. LOTS OF TEARING, DIPPING AND SHARING. THE FETA GOES ALL RICH AND SQUIDGY IN THE OVEN, IT IS SUBLIME.

BAKED FETA, CHERRY TOMATOES & GARLIC CIABATTA

01 Preheat your oven to 160°C fan (180°C/360°F/Gas Mark 4).

02 Roughly chop your onion and a garlic clove up.

03 Mix the cherry tomatoes, pitted olives, 4 teaspoons of capers, the chopped onion and garlic, a heaped teaspoon of oregano, a drizzle of olive oil, salt and pepper in a bowl.

04 Put the feta blocks on a layer of foil on a baking tray, folding the edges of the foil up to collect the juices. Pile your mixture on top. Bake for 30 minutes. When it has baked for 20 minutes, place your ciabatta loaf in the oven to warm up.

05 Meanwhile, chop up 4 garlic cloves and a handful of parsley leaves and add to a bowl. Melt 150 g (1 stick plus 2 tablespoons) butter in a pan and then add to the garlic and parsley. Mix it in.

06 Cut your warm ciabatta in half. Spread your butter all over the two cut sides, and then place back in the oven for 5 minutes.

07 Remove the feta from the oven. Garnish with parsley. Tear up your garlic ciabatta, spoon out the feta and tuck in!

Damn Sam The Miracle Man
Damn Sam The Miracle Man

CARAMELIZED ONION & AVOCADO INGREDIENTS

butter
4 eggs
265-g (9-oz) packet of gouda
4 bagels
caramelized onion chutney
2 avocados
rocket (arugula)

HALLOUMI & MINT INGREDIENTS

225-g (8-oz) block of halloumi
fresh mint
plain yogurt
1 lemon
4 bagels
sundried tomato paste
rocket (arugula)

THE PERFECT SPEEDY BRUNCH FOR AFTER A HEAVY NIGHT OUT. FOLDING THE OMELETTE INTO A PARCEL FOR THE CARAMELIZED ONION & AVOCADO BAGEL LETS THE GOUDA GET NICE AND GOOEY.

ULTIMATE BRUNCH BAGELS (2 WAYS)

CARAMELIZED ONION & AVOCADO

01 Heat a teaspoonful of butter in a frying pan (skillet) until it foams slightly. Crack an egg into a bowl and beat, then season with salt and pepper. Pour the beaten egg into a pan and leave to cook a thin omelette.

02 Slice the gouda and add a generous sprinkle to the middle of the omelette. Fold the omelette in so that you create a little parcel. Repeat for the other three eggs.

03 Toast the bagels, then spread the caramelized onion chutney (as much as you like, to taste).

04 Place an omelette on top of the chutney, then add some more gouda, some slices of avocado and a handful of rocket for good measure. Enjoy!

HALLOUMI & MINT

01 Slice up the block of halloumi and season with a bit of salt and pepper. Whack some olive oil in a pan and fry the halloumi slices until crispy and brown.

02 Remove the mint leaves from their stalks. Chop up the mint leaves finely and stick them in a bowl. Add 4 tablespoons of plain yogurt and squeeze in the juice of a lemon. Mix.

03 Toast the bagels. Spread some sundried tomato paste on the bottom, then layer the halloumi, yogurt dressing and a handful of rocket. Repeat for the other bagels and serve!

HEALTHY INGREDIENTS

rolled (old-fashioned) oats
almond milk
coconut milk
chia seeds
maple syrup
fresh strawberries

BIRCHER INGREDIENTS

jumbo oats
1 red apple
1 green apple
ground cinnamon
almond milk
apple juice (not from concentrate)
almonds
2 bananas
dairy-free coconut yogurt

THESE OATS ARE RIDICULOUSLY EASY TO DO AND A GREAT RECIPE TO HAVE UP YOUR SLEEVE. YOU CAN ADD WHATEVER YOU LIKE, DIFFERENT FRUITS, DIFFERENT NUTS. HAVE FUN AND MAKE IT YOUR OWN.

VEGAN OVERNIGHT OATS (2 WAYS) [VG]

FOR THE HEALTHY MOB

01   Mix 200 g (2 cups) rolled oats, 240 ml (1 cup) almond milk, 240 ml (1 cup) coconut milk, 2 tablespoons chia seeds and 3–4 tablespoons maple syrup in a large bowl.

02   Chop 250 g/9 oz strawberries, then fold them into the mixture, setting a few aside for garnishing.

03   Cover, then put in the fridge overnight or for at least 4 hours.

04   When ready, divide into 4 cups and top with the leftover strawberries for texture.

FOR THE BIRCHER-LOVING MOB

01   Pour 3 mugs of oats into a bowl. Grate your apples and add to the oats. Add 2 heaped teaspoons of cinnamon, then pour in 560 ml (1 pint) of almond milk and the same of apple juice.

02   Mix everything together, cover in clingfilm (plastic wrap), then put the bowl in the fridge overnight.

03   The next morning, chop 100 g (¾ cup) of almonds and add them into the bowl with the oats. Mix everything together, then divide it into bowls. Put a semi-circle of banana slices around the edge of the bowl, and spoon on a big dollop of yogurt over the top. Add a pinch of cinnamon, and tuck in!

2

FRESH MOB

INGREDIENTS

green lentils
quinoa
tahini
2 lemons
garlic
red wine vinegar
Dijon mustard
250-g (9-oz) packet of cherry
tomatoes
1 cucumber
1 gem lettuce
1 avocado
fresh coriander (cilantro)
fennel seeds
parsley
olive oil
salt and pepper

THIS IS TEXTURE COMBO MADE IN HEAVEN – CRUNCHY SALAD WITH A RICH, SMOOTH HUMMUS BASE. I GOT INSPIRATION FOR THIS DISH FROM A LUNCH SPOT IN PARIS, AND I'M SO EXCITED FOR YOU ALL TO TRY IT!

QUINOA SALAD WITH GREEN LENTIL HUMMUS BASE [VG]

01 Rinse 250 g (1½ cups) of green lentils and cook according to the instructions on the packet.

02 At the same time, cook 250 g (1½ cups) of quinoa according to the packet instructions. Fluff and set aside to cool.

03 Add your cooked lentils, 80 ml (⅓ cup) of olive oil, 60 ml (¼ cup) of water, 180 g (¾ cup) of tahini, the juice of a lemon, a garlic clove and some salt to a food processor and blend until creamy and smooth. Add more olive oil or water to thin out if necessary.

04 Dressing time. Whisk 4 tablespoons of red wine vinegar, 2 tablespoons of Dijon mustard, a pinch of salt and a good grinding of pepper. Slowly add 80 ml (⅓ cup) of olive oil to the mixture whilst whisking. Then add the juice of a lemon.

05 Halve the cherry tomatoes, and chop up the cucumber, gem lettuce and avocado. Finely chop the coriander.

06 Mix together the salad veggies and quinoa, and pour over a cup of the dressing. Toss together.

07 Create a green lentil hummus base, then add the salad on top. Enjoy!

INGREDIENTS

fresh ginger
red miso paste
200-g (7-oz) bag of purple
sprouting broccoli
vermicelli noodles
beansprouts
3 limes
soy sauce
fresh coriander (cilantro)
1 cucumber
1 red chilli
salted peanuts
olive oil

**THE ROASTED MISO
BROCOLLI. THE
SALT PEANUTS. THE
ZINGY DRESSING. ALL
COMING TOGETHER
TO FORM ONE OF THE
MOST SPECTACULAR
MOUTHFULS YOU'RE EVER
LIKELY TO TAKE.**

VIETNAMESE
VERMICELLI BOWL [VG]

01 Preheat your oven to 180°C fan (200°C/400°F/Gas Mark 6).

02 Finely chop a 2.5-cm (1-inch) piece of ginger. Mix 1½ tablespoons of miso paste with some olive oil in a bowl. If necessary, add up to 50 ml (3 tablespoons) of water to loosen the mixture.

03 Wash your broccoli and place on a roasting tray, then baste with the miso mixture. Let it roast in the oven for 30 minutes.

04 Meanwhile, cook 400 g (14 oz) of vermicelli according to the packet instructions. Drain and rinse with cold water until the noodles are cold.

05 Wash your beansprouts and lightly pan-fry with a glug of oil until slightly wilted. Set to the side to cool.

06 Dressing time. Take 3 limes and use a teaspoon to get all the juice out. Add 2 teaspoons of soy sauce. Chop up a handful of coriander and mix.

07 Chop up your cucumber into circles and then cut the circles into halves.

08 De-seed your red chillies and finely chop them. Chop up another handful of coriander.

09 Assemble your bowls with vermicelli and beansprouts, then pour a generous amount of dressing on top of it, top with cucumber, chilli, coriander and crushed salted peanuts.

INGREDIENTS

220 g (8 oz) tenderstem
broccoli (broccolini)
400 g (2¼ cups) brown rice
tahini
sesame oil
1 lemon
1 mango
pickled ginger
salted peanuts
sesame seeds

WE SPENT A LONG
TIME DEVELOPING A
COMPLETELY VEGAN POKE
BOWL, AND HERE IT IS.
A BITE OF THE TAHINI-
DRESSED GRIDDLED
TENDERSTEM BROCCOLI
IS LIKE DYING AND GOING
TO HEAVEN. SHOUT OUT
TO ISLAND POKE FOR
THE INSPIRATION.

POKE BOWL WITH GRIDDLED TAHINI TENDERSTEM BROCCOLI [] [VG]

01 Chop the tenderstem broccoli into bite-sized pieces. Add to a pan of boiling water and boil for 4 minutes. Drain.

02 Get the brown rice on (follow the instructions on the packet).

03 Heat a griddle (ridged stovetop) pan. Add the broccoli to the pan. Cook until charred. Remove and set aside.

04 Dressing time. Add 3 tablespoons of tahini, a teaspoon of sesame oil and the juice of a lemon into a bowl. Add water and mix until you have a creamy consistency.

05 Add the broccoli to the dressing and toss it around.

06 Once the rice is ready, drain, and then add 2 teaspoons of sesame oil to it. Toss it in.

07 Cut the mango into chunks.

08 Serving time. Fill the bottom of 4 bowls with rice. Add equal portions of broccoli and mango chunks to each bowl. Finish with a handful of pickled ginger in each bowl.

09 Bash up some salted peanuts and scatter them on top, along with some sesame seeds. Dig your fork in and enjoy!

SERVES 4
1 hr

The Gene Dudley Group
Inspector Norse

INGREDIENTS

2 (bell) peppers
pine nuts
fresh basil
1 lemon
garlic
veggie Parmesan
3 courgettes (zucchini)
225-g (8-oz) packet of halloumi
plain (all-purpose) flour
2 eggs
dried breadcrumbs
250-g (9-oz) packet of cherry
tomatoes
rocket (arugula)
olive oil
vegetable oil
salt and pepper

HALLOUMI CROUTONS – THE GREATEST INVENTION SINCE SLICED BREAD. CRUNCHY OUTSIDE, WITH THAT BEAUTIFUL SOFT HALLOUMI BITE ON THE INSIDE. LEAVE THE HALLOUMI TO COOK UNTIL THE BREADCRUMBS ARE A DEEP BROWN.

HALLOUMI CROUTON SUPER SALAD [★]

01   Preheat your oven to 180°C fan (200°C/400°F/Gas Mark 6).

02   Cut your peppers into chunks. Add to a roasting tray with salt, pepper and a drizzle of olive oil. Roast for 40 minutes or until charred and soft.

03   Pesto time. First toast 50 g (scant ½ cup) pine nuts in a dry frying pan (skillet). Into a blender add 20 g (scant ¼ cup) of the toasted pine nuts, a handful of basil leaves, the juice of a lemon, 1 garlic clove and 50 g (¾ cup) Parmesan. Add 5 tablespoons of olive oil and blend until smooth.

04   Courgette time. Cut your courgettes into thin strips. Drizzle with olive oil, salt and pepper. Add to a hot griddle (ridged stovetop) pan and cook for 5–6 minutes on each side.

05   Halloumi time. Cut your halloumi into small cubes. Get 3 bowls out. Add flour to one, 2 eggs to another (whisk them up) and breadcrumbs to the third. Dip your halloumi in the flour, then the eggs, then the breadcrumbs.

06   Get a pan on the heat. Fill it up 2 cm (¾ inch) high with vegetable oil. Heat the oil, and then add the croutons to the pan. Cook for 3–4 minutes until golden brown.

07   Remove the croutons from the heat and place them on some kitchen paper.

08   Halve your cherry tomatoes.

09   Add all of your ingredients, along with a bag of rocket and the leftover pine nuts, to a large salad bowl. Pour over your pesto dressing, toss it all together and serve it up.

INGREDIENTS

4 red (bell) peppers
garlic
1 lemon
flaked (slivered) almonds
sherry vinegar
tomato purée (paste)
500 g (1 lb 2 oz) dried
pappardelle
Kalamata olives
fresh basil
olive oil
salt and pepper

ROMESCO SAUCE – A
NUT-BASED CATALAN
RECIPE. IT'S SAVOURY,
RICH FLAVOUR WORKS
PERFECTLY WITH PASTA
AND SOME SALTY
KALAMATA OLIVES. A
GREAT SIMPLE PASTA
DISH TO ADD TO
YOUR REPERTOIRE.

ROMESCO PAPPARDELLE WITH KALAMATA OLIVES

01 Preheat your oven to 160°C fan (180°C/360°F/Gas Mark 4).

02 Add the red peppers and 3 garlic cloves (skin on) to a roasting tray with a lemon cut in half. Roast for 45 minutes.

03 Once the peppers are soft, add them to a blender. Squeeze in the roasted garlic and roast lemon juice. Add 2 tablespoons of flaked almonds, 2 tablespoons of sherry vinegar, a tablespoon of tomato purée, salt, pepper and 3 tablespoons of olive oil. Blitz until smooth.

04 Get the pasta on.

05 Once the pasta is al dente, drain (save some of the pasta water). Add back to the pan with your Romesco sauce, a large handful of chopped Kalamata olives and a handful of torn basil. Serve the pasta into bowls, garnish with leftover basil and enjoy!

BABA GANOUSH PITTAS

SERVES 4
1 hr 10 mins

Junodream
Fire Doors

INGREDIENTS

3 aubergines (eggplants)
garlic
3 beetroot (beets)
1 carrot
fresh mint
fresh coriander (cilantro)
225-g (8-oz) packet of halloumi
tahini
2 lemons
8 pittas
salt and pepper

01 Preheat your oven to 180°C fan (200°C/400°F/Gas Mark 6).

02 Add the whole aubergines to a baking tray. Add 2 garlic cloves to the tray (in their skins).

03 Cook for an hour, making sure the aubergines are cooked all the way through.

04 While the aubergines are cooking, grate your beetroot and a carrot. Chop up a handful each of mint and coriander and mix into the grated veg.

05 Slice your halloumi and pan-fry it, letting the slices get crisp and brown.

06 Remove the aubergines from the oven. Slice them open and scoop out the soft flesh. Squeeze out the roasted garlic from their skins. Put the aubergine flesh and garlic into a food processor with 2 tablespoons of tahini, the juice of a lemon, and salt and pepper. Process until smooth.

07 Toast your pittas. Spread a dollop of baba ganoush on the inside of each pitta, stuff it with halloumi slices and grated veg, and squeeze some lemon juice to top it off.

BABA GANOUSH –
PROBABLY ONE OF THE
BEST THINGS IN THE
WORLD. SOFT, GARLICKY,
SMOKEY AUBERGINE. IT
GOES WITH JUST ABOUT
ANYTHING. WE HAVE
DECIDED TO STUFF IT
INSIDE A PITTA WITH A
CRUNCHY SALAD FOR THE
ULTIMATE SANDWICH.

SERVES 4
25 mins

Bumblebee Unlimited
Lady Bug

INGREDIENTS

200-g (7-oz) packet of
soba noodles
250-g (9-oz) packet of
portobello mushrooms
soy sauce
2 carrots
½ red cabbage
1 red (bell) pepper
1 lime
sriracha
sesame oil
17-g (1-oz) packet of nori
seaweed
coriander (cilantro)
olive oil

SOBA NOODLE SALAD WITH CHARRED PORTOBELLO MUSHROOMS [VG]

01 Cook the soba noodles according to the packet instructions. Drain and rinse with cold water (to stop them overcooking).

02 Finely slice the portobello mushrooms and add to a frying pan (skillet) with a splash of olive oil. Add a tablespoon of soy sauce, and cook the mushrooms until they begin to char. Remove from the heat.

03 Grate the carrots and red cabbage, and finely slice a red pepper. Mix with the noodles.

04 Sauce time. Whisk together 2 tablespoons of soy sauce, the juice of a lime and a tablespoon of sriracha. Add 3 tablespoons of sesame oil while whisking.

05 Combine the dressing and the noodles, top with mushrooms and sprinkle over the nori seaweed (broken into little pieces) and a handful of chopped coriander.

THIS IS DEFINITELY ONE
FOR THE HEALTHY MOB
– SOBA NOODLES ARE
SAINTLY. MAKE SURE YOU
LEAVE THE MUSHROOMS
COOKING UNTIL THEY
ARE DARK AND GNARLY –
THEY BRING THE DEPTH OF
FLAVOUR HERE.

SERVES 4

1 hr 10 mins

Manfred Mann Chapter Three

One Way Glass

INGREDIENTS

12 new potatoes (big ones)

2 red (bell) peppers

1 red onion

2 lemons

2 corn on the cob

garlic

dried oregano

red wine vinegar

2 hot red chillies

200-g (7-oz) block of feta

400-g (14-oz) tin of black beans

½ cucumber

fresh coriander (cilantro)

olive oil

salt and pepper

IF YOU THOUGHT YOU COULDN'T EAT PERI-PERI OUTSIDE OF PORTUGAL, YOU'RE VERY, VERY WRONG. WE HAVE PERFECTED OUR RECIPE, WHICH WORKS PERFECTLY ON TOP OF THESE CRISPY HASSELBACK POTATOES.

HASSELBACK POTATOES WITH PERI PERI DRESSING & FETA

01 Preheat your oven to 180°C fan (200°C/400°F/Gas Mark 6).

02 Prep the potatoes. Carefully make small vertical slits, 2 mm/ ½ inch apart, three-quarters of the way down each potato, all the way along.

03 Add the potatoes to a roasting tray. Drizzle with olive oil and season well with salt and pepper.

04 Add to the oven and roast for 50 minutes or until golden and crispy.

05 Peri peri time. In another roasting tray add 2 de-seeded, roughly sliced red peppers, 1 sliced red onion and 1 lemon (halved, cut-side down). Drizzle with olive oil and add the tray to the oven for 45 minutes.

06 Add your corn to another tray, drizzle with olive oil, salt and pepper and roast in the oven for 30 minutes, turning every 10 minutes.

07 Once the potatoes are nice and crispy, remove them from the oven and set aside.

08 Peri peri sauce time. Add your roasted peppers, onion and pulp from the lemon to a blender. Add 2 grated garlic cloves, 2 teaspoons of oregano, 1½ tablespoons of red wine vinegar, salt, pepper and a drizzle of olive oil. Add the zest and juice of a fresh lemon.

09 Load the potatoes with the sauce and add crumbled feta, black beans and ½ a de-seeded, sliced cucumber. Scatter chopped coriander on top and serve up.

INGREDIENTS

4 (bell) peppers (not green)
fresh coriander (cilantro)
fresh parsley
red wine vinegar
1 red chilli
3 shallots
dried oregano
garlic
650-g (1 lb 7-oz) packet of new
potatoes
manchego
olive oil
salt and pepper

**THIS DISH IS MORE OF AN
ASSEMBLY THAN A RECIPE
– ALL THE ELEMENTS
JUST WORK SO WELL
TOGETHER. THE SALTY
MANCHEGO SHAVINGS
ON THE TOP MAKE
THE DIFFERENCE.**

SIMPLE CHIMICHURRI, ROASTED PEPPER & NEW POTATO SALAD

01 Preheat your oven to 160°C fan (180°C/360°F/Gas Mark 4).

02 Quarter the peppers and add to a roasting tray. Season with salt and pepper and drizzle with olive oil. Add the tray to the oven for 45 minutes.

03 Chimichurri time. Add a large handful of chopped coriander and chopped parsley to a bowl. Add 4 tablespoons of red wine vinegar, 1 finely chopped red chilli, 7 tablespoons of olive oil, 3 chopped shallots, a heaped teaspoon of oregano, and salt and pepper. Add a grated garlic clove and mix everything together. It should be the consistency of pesto, so add more herbs if needed.

04 Bring a pan of water to the boil. Add a large pinch of salt and then add your potatoes. Cook until almost soft.

05 Once cooked, drain, and then add salt, pepper and olive oil to the potatoes.

06 Serving time. Into a bowl add some roasted peppers, some potatoes, and cover with a few large dollops of chimichurri. Shave manchego over the top and tuck in!

INGREDIENTS

4 red or yellow (bell) peppers
ciabatta
chilli (hot red pepper) flakes
garlic
4 beef tomatoes
2 mozzarella balls
balsamic vinegar
fresh basil
olive oil
sea salt and pepper

**A NAUGHTY, NAUGHTY
LITTLE SALAD. IDEAL
FOR THE LONG SUMMER
EVENINGS. THE GARLIC
CROUTONS ARE GREAT
AND CAN BE USED TO
ELEVATE ALL OF
YOUR SALLYS.**

TOMATO & ROASTED PEPPER SUMMER SALAD

01 Preheat your oven to 180°C fan (200°C/400°F/Gas Mark 6).

02 Slice 4 red or yellow peppers into thin strips and season with salt and pepper.

03 Place on a lined baking tray, drizzle with olive oil and roast in the preheated oven for 15–20 minutes.

04 Cut a small loaf of ciabatta into small chunks. Add to a baking tray. Drizzle with olive oil. Add 2 teaspoons of chilli flakes and 2 crushed garlic cloves and mix around. Roast for 30 minutes until a deep golden brown.

05 Slice the tomatoes and tear 2 mozzarella balls into big chunks.

06 Combine in a large bowl and add a large glug of olive oil, salt and pepper and a smaller glug of balsamic vinegar. Mix well.

07 Add the peppers and croutons to the tomato and mozzarella mixture. Mix well.

08 Serve your fresh salad into bowls and sprinkle your crunchy croutons on top. Garnish with fresh basil leaves and a pinch of sea salt.

3

SPEEDY
MOB

VEGGIE SATAY NOODLES

SERVES 4
20 mins

Metronomy
The Look

INGREDIENTS

3 (bell) peppers
2 carrots
sesame oil
400-g (14-oz) packet of egg
noodles
6 spring onions (scallions)
1 lime
peanut butter
400-g (14-oz) tin of
coconut milk
soy sauce
fresh coriander (cilantro)
peanuts
vegetable oil
salt and pepper

01 Chop your peppers and carrots into matchsticks. Add them to a wok with a splash of vegetable oil. Cook on high so they start charring. Once the vegetables are charred but still firm, remove them from the heat. Add them to a bowl and add 1½ teaspoons of sesame oil to them.

02 Get the egg noodles on in a separate pan and cook according to the packet instructions.

03 Finely chop your spring onions and add them to a bowl. Squeeze over the juice of a lime and add a big pinch of salt. Scrunch everything together – this will pickle the spring onions and take away the strong flavour.

04 Back to the wok. First, wipe out the excess oil. Then add a tablespoon of peanut butter, the coconut milk and 4 tablespoons of soy sauce. Mix everything together and bubble over a high heat until you have a nice thick sauce.

05 Drain the noodles and pour them into the wok. Add the sesame vegetables, and stir everything together.

06 Tip in your spring onions, add a teaspoon more of sesame oil and mix everything together. Scatter in some coriander and peanuts, and serve up!

DONE IN ABOUT 20
MINUTES, SO A PERFECT
MID-WEEK SUPPER. MAKE
SURE YOU SCRUNCH YOUR
SPRING ONIONS TO GET
THEM PICKLING – THIS
SPEEDY LIMEY PICKLE
BRINGS THE FRESH KICK
THAT IS NEEDED.

PERI PERI HALLOUMI BURGERS [★]

SERVES 4

1 hr

Donnell Pitman

Love Explosion

INGREDIENTS

3 (bell) peppers (not green)

1 red onion

½ lemon

smoked paprika

dried oregano

red wine vinegar

red chilli

garlic

01   Preheat your oven to 180°C fan (200°C/400°F/Gas Mark 6).

02   Cut 3 peppers and 1 red onion into chunks. Add them to a baking tray. Add ½ a lemon, face down, into the tray. Place the tray in the preheated oven for 45 minutes.

03   Once the peppers are beginning to char, remove tray. Add one-third of the pepper and onion mixture and the pulp of the roast lemon to a blender, with a teaspoon each of smoked paprika and oregano. Add 1 tablespoon of red wine vinegar, a red chilli and a garlic clove. Season with salt and pepper and add a tablespoon of olive oil. Blitz until smooth.

04   Slice your halloumi then get it on a hot griddle (ridged stovetop) pan. Cook for 3–4 minutes on each side.

05   Toast 4 burger buns.

2 x 225-g (8-oz) packs
of halloumi
4 burger buns
mayo
bag of salad
olive oil
salt and pepper

06 Mix your blitzed peri peri sauce with 5 tablespoons of mayonnaise.

07 Assembly time. Take a bun. Add a layer of peri peri mayo. Then some halloumi, followed by some of the roasted peppers, some salad, more mayo, more halloumi and then top it with the bun lid. Tuck in and enjoy!

THE FRESHEST VEGGIE BURGER ABOUT. THE PERI PERI MAYO IS EVERYTHING – LATHER IT ON GENEROUSLY!

INGREDIENTS

150-g (5½-oz) packet of
portobello mushrooms
1 brown onion
1 carrot
white cabbage
5 spring onions (scallions)
125-g (4-oz) packet of fresh
shiitake mushrooms
400-g (14-oz) packet of wok-
ready udon noodles
soy sauce
mirin
sesame oil
vegetable oil
black pepper

**A RESTAURANT CLASSIC
THAT IS SO SIMPLE TO DO
AT HOME YOURSELVES.
MIRIN IS KEY IN THIS
DISH – YOU MAY HAVE
TO GO TO A BIGGER OR
SPECIALIST STORE TO
FIND IT, BUT IT IS
ESSENTIAL AND WORTH
THE EFFORT. IT IS
JAPANESE RICE WINE, AND
BRINGS THE EDGE.**

YASAI YAKI UDON NOODLES [ ] [VG]

01 Slice up the portobello mushrooms. Finely chop a brown onion. Cut a carrot into matchsticks. Shred ⅓ of a white cabbage. Finely slice 3 spring onions.

02 Into a pan add 2 tablespoons of sesame oil and 2 tablespoons of vegetable oil.

03 Add your carrot, cabbage and onion. Allow them to soften for 2–3 minutes, and then throw in your portobello mushrooms.

04 Cook for another minute, then add your shiitake mushrooms. Mix everything in, and cook for another 2 minutes.

05 At this point, add your 3 sliced spring onions. Cook for another 2 minutes, and then add the udon noodles. Season with pepper, and then add 4 tablespoons of soy sauce and 2 tablespoons of mirin.

06 Mix everything together, cook for another minute and then you're all set. Remove from the heat, and serve while hot. Garnish with a couple of sliced spring onions and enjoy!

SERVES 4
15 mins

Hailu Mergia
Tizita

INGREDIENTS

500-g (1 lb 2-oz) packet of
gnocchi
250-g (9-oz) packet of
chestnut mushrooms
garlic
fresh rosemary
fresh thyme
1 lemon
crème fraîche or sour cream
(we use Elmlea)
200-g (7-oz) packet of goat's
cheese
salted butter
salt and pepper

**MAKE SURE YOU ONLY
SOAK THE GNOCCHI
IN WATER INSTEAD OF
BOILING IT. THIS MEANS
IT WON'T OVERCOOK IN
THE OVEN AND WILL HOLD
ITS SHAPE. TALEGGIO IS
THE ULTIMATE CHEESY
TOPPING HERE – LEAVE IT
UNDER THE GRILL UNTIL
NICE AND GOLDEN.**

CREAMY MUSHROOM GNOCCHI WITH GOAT'S CHEESE

01 Put a large pot of water on to boil, add a generous amount of salt and cook the gnocchi according to the packet instructions.

02 Thinly slice the chestnut mushrooms.

03 Melt a tablespoon of butter in a large frying pan (skillet) over a medium heat.

04 Add the sliced mushrooms and cook until soft (3–5 minutes). At this point, add the garlic and a small handful of rosemary and thyme leaves, and the zest of half a lemon. Cook for another minute.

05 Add a tablespoon of crème fraîche. Stir it through the mushrooms.

06 Squeeze in 10 drops of freshly squeezed lemon juice.

07 When your gnocchi's cooked, drain and add to your sauce.

08 Dollop the goat's cheese over the top. Season well with black pepper and serve.

INGREDIENTS

1 brown onion
garlic
fresh ginger
tomato purée (paste)
ground cumin
paprika
chilli (hot red pepper) flakes
400 g (2 cups) split red lentils
400-g (14-oz) tin of
coconut milk
spinach
400 g (2 cups) basmati rice

SPICY COCONUT LENTIL DAHL [VG]

01 Chop up your onion, 3 garlic cloves and a thumb-sized piece of ginger.

02 Pan-fry the onion, ginger and garlic. When soft, add a heaped tablespoon of tomato purée (paste) and 1 teaspoon of ground cumin, 1 teaspoon of paprika and 1 teaspoon of chilli flakes. Fry for a couple of minutes to release their aromas.

03 Add the lentils and coconut milk, and bring to the boil, then simmer for 1 hour, adding water when necessary and stirring frequently.

04 Stir in some spinach right at the end.

05 Get the basmati rice on and cook according to the instructions on the packet.

06 Serve the dahl over rice.

THE IS AN ULTIMATE WINTER WARMER. I HAVE ALWAYS BEEN A BIT SCEPTICAL ABOUT LENTILS, BUT THEY ARE THE ABSOLUTE HERO IN THIS DISH. SO RICH. SO WARMING. GIVE IT A GO...

15-MINUTE LAKSA [VG]

SERVES 4
15 mins

Rahaan
Make Me Hot

INGREDIENTS

ground coriander
paprika
ground cumin
4 red chillies
1 brown onion
2 lemongrass stalks
fresh ginger
garlic

01 Make the paste first – add 1 teaspoon each of ground coriander, paprika and ground cumin to a pan and heat until fragrant (one minute or so). Add to a food processor with 4 red chillies, a roughly chopped brown onion, 2 lemongrass stalks (white part only), a small grated piece of ginger, 2 garlic cloves and a glug of oil.

02 Add the paste to a saucepan and fry for a few minutes.

03 Meanwhile, finely slice 2 carrots and slice 2 courgettes.

04 Add your vegetables and coconut milk to the pan and bring to the boil, then add 150 g (5½ oz) rice noodles. Cook until the rice noodles are soft.

05 Turn off the heat, add a handful of chopped coriander and squeeze a lime on top.

06 Serve up and enjoy!

2 carrots
2 courgettes (zucchini)
2 x 400-g (14-oz) tins of
coconut milk
rice noodles
sugar snap peas
fresh coriander (cilantro)
1 lime
vegetable oil

MAKING YOUR OWN LAKSA PASTA IS THE EASIEST THING TO DO AND PACKS SO MUCH MORE FLAVOUR THAN THE STORE-BOUGHT STUFF. DONE IN MINUTES – GIVE IT A SPIN AND IMPRESS YOUR MOB.

**SO GOOD ITS ALMOST AS
IF I HAD A RAT IN MY HAT
WHEN I WAS MAKING IT...**

QUICK LENTIL RATATOUILLE [VG]

01 Finely dice the onion and 2 carrots, add to a pan with a glug of olive oil and cook until the onions are soft and translucent. Then add 2 aubergines and 2 courgettes, both cut into rough cubes. Cook down until the aubergines and courgettes start to char.

02 Finely chop 3 garlic cloves, add and stir well. Once soft, add your tins of tomatoes. Cook for 8 minutes over a medium heat.

03 Add 350 g (2 cups) rinsed Puy lentils, 500 ml (2 cups) of water, 1 teaspoon of oregano, ½ teaspoon of thyme, 1 teaspoon of ground coriander, and salt and pepper. Simmer over a low heat for 20 minutes, stirring frequently to ensure the lentils are not sticking. Add water if and when necessary.

04 Once you have a delicious, thick ratatouille, add a handful of fresh basil. Serve in bowls with salt and pepper sprinkled on top.

PUMPKIN PASTA [VG]

SERVES 4
45 mins

The Kinks
Victoria

INGREDIENTS

1 pumpkin
1 sweet potato
garlic
2 red onions
500-g (1 lb 2-oz) packet of
dried spaghetti
3 leeks
olive oil
salt and pepper

PUMPKIN AND LEEKS – A MATCH MADE IN HEAVEN. THE TRICK WITH LEEKS IS TO COOK THEM ON A LOW-MEDIUM HEAT SO THEY GET REALLY NICE AND SILKY WITHOUT CATCHING ON THE PAN.

01 Preheat your oven to 200°C fan (220°C/425°F/Gas Mark 7).

02 Cut your pumpkin up, de-seed it and put it on a roasting tray with some olive oil, salt and pepper.

03 Wash and cut the sweet potato, 2 garlic cloves and the onions, then place in a separate roasting tray with olive oil, salt and pepper.

04 Roast for around 30 minutes, making sure to take out the garlic as soon as it looks caramelized because it tends to burn.

05 Meanwhile, boil the pasta according to the packet instructions.

06 Wash and cut the leeks, then pan-fry with olive oil and a generous amount of salt.

07 Back to the roasted vegetables. Place all of it into a blender and blend until smooth. Combine the pasta and blended sauce in a pan, making sure the sauce covers all the pasta. Serve with a glug of olive oil and a spoonful of leeks!

INGREDIENTS

5 shallots
3 red chillies
paprika
fresh ginger
fresh coriander (cilantro)
2 limes
garlic
lemongrass purée
400 g (2¼ cups) basmati rice
(we use Tilda)
1 large carrot
2 red (bell) peppers
400-ml (14-oz) tin of
coconut milk
peanut butter
olive oil

**SACK THOSE SHOP
BOUGHT PASTES FOREVER
– THIS IS THE WAY
FORWARD. IF POSSIBLE,
USE PEANUT BUTTER MADE
FROM PEANUTS ONLY –
THE BEST STUFF REALLY
TAKES THIS DISH TO THE
NEXT LEVEL.**

30-MINUTE PEANUT RED THAI CURRY BOWLS [VG]

01 First, make your curry sauce. Into a blender add the shallots, chillies, 3 teaspoons of paprika, a peeled and chopped 5-cm (2-inch) piece of ginger, a handful of fresh coriander including stalks, the juice of a lime (use a teaspoon to get all the juice out), 2 cloves of garlic and 3 heaped teaspoons of lemongrass purée. Blitz until smooth.

02 Get the basmati rice on (follow the instructions on the packet).

03 Chop up your carrot and peppers.

04 In a pan, add a glug of olive oil and throw in your chopped carrots and chopped red peppers.

05 When mostly cooked through, add your curry sauce. Mix thoroughly.

06 Add your coconut milk and allow it to simmer so that the sauce thickens.

07 When your sauce is thick enough, add 2 heaped teaspoons of peanut butter and fold it in.

08 Serve on a bed of rice and top with fresh coriander and a squeeze of lime.

RAINBOW DRAGON NOODLES

SERVES 4
30 mins

MR Given Raw
Boogie Magic

INGREDIENTS

4 courgettes (zucchini)
2 carrots
1 red cabbage
2 red (bell) peppers
sriracha
soy sauce
sugar
4 eggs
unsalted cashews
fresh coriander (cilantro)
vegetable oil
salt

A HEALTHY NOODLE OPTION – PACKED FULL OF VEGGIES. A GREAT LIGHT DINNER. ADD COOKED DRIED NOODLES IF YOU WANT TO BULK IT OUT!

01 Spiralize the courgettes and carrots. Finely slice a red cabbage and 2 red peppers.

02 Sauce time. In a bowl, mix together 5 teaspoons of sriracha, 4 tablespoons of soy sauce and a teaspoon of sugar. Set to the side.

03 Add all the veg to a frying pan (skillet) with a good glug of oil. Fry for 1 minute, and then add 4 beaten eggs to the pan.

04 Let cook until the egg starts to form around the veggie noodles and then mix well. Add the sauce!

05 In a separate frying pan, toast some unsalted cashews with some salt.

06 Serve the noodles with toasted cashews and some chopped coriander.

FUSS-FREE MOB

4

INGREDIENTS

1 cucumber
1 red (bell) pepper
1 green pepper
garlic
3 spring onions (scallions)
1 stale bread roll
14 plum tomatoes
sherry vinegar
olive oil
salt and pepper
ice

SACK OFF THE CARTON STUFF. THIS RECIPE IS THE BUSINESS – AND SO, SO REFRESHING. GET SOME NICE TOMATOES.

HOMEMADE GAZPACHO [★] [VG]

01 Prep time. Peel, de-seed and slice 1 cucumber. De-seed 1 red and 1 green pepper, and chop into chunks. Chop 1½ garlic cloves into thin slices. Slice up 3 spring onions. Tear up a stale bread roll.

02 Throw all these ingredients into a large bowl. Add the plum tomatoes, 3½ tablespoons of sherry vinegar, 5 tablespoons of olive oil and a generous sprinkle of salt and pepper.

03 Get your hands stuck in and crush everything into a pulp. Once it is broken down, get the blender involved.

04 Blend until smooth, and then ladle the gazpacho into a pouring jug (pitcher).

05 Serve with lots of ice, a drizzle of good olive oil on top at the end, and a bit of pepper. Enjoy!

ONE-POT VEGGIE SOUPS (4 WAYS)

SERVES 4

Mary Clark
Take Me I'm Yours

ALL 4 OF THESE SOUP OPTIONS ARE RIDICULOUSLY SIMPLE. APART FROM A BIT OF ROASTING, THEY ARE ALL DONE IN ONE POT. SO MINIMAL WASHING UP. THEY ARE GREAT FOR FREEZING AS WELL SO COOK IN BATCHES AND SAVE FOR A RAINY DAY.

CARROT & CORIANDER

INGREDIENTS

1 brown onion
ground coriander
10 carrots
vegetable stock (bouillon) cube
fresh coriander (cilantro)
chilli (hot red pepper) flakes
1 lime
olive oil
salt and pepper

01 Glug some olive oil into a large saucepan, add a chopped onion and fry until soft and translucent. Add 1 teaspoon of ground coriander and fry for a minute. Season with salt and pepper.

02 Peel and chop up 10 carrots roughly. Add the carrots, a stock cube and 1 litre (4 cups) of water to the pan and simmer for 30 minutes over a medium heat (or until the carrots are fully cooked).

03 Take the soup off the heat. Add a large handful of fresh coriander and decant the mixture into a blender. Blitz until smooth.

04 Add 2 teaspoons of chilli flakes and the juice of a lime, and mix in. Serve with another squeeze of lime juice on top.

COCONUT & TOMATO

INGREDIENTS

2 red onions
6 tomatoes
garlic
400-g (14-oz) tin of
coconut milk
tomato purée (paste)
olive oil
salt and pepper

01 Preheat your oven to 180°C fan (200°C/400°F/Gas Mark 6).

02 Chop up 2 red onions and tomatoes roughly.

03 Prepare a garlic bulb for roasting. Cut the top off, wrap in tin foil, pour a generous amount of olive oil over then close the tin foil.

04 Place everything in a roasting tray and roast for 1 hour. The onions may need only 45 minutes (remove when cooked and starting to blacken).

05 Add the onions, tomatoes, roasted garlic flesh, coconut milk and a tablespoon of tomato purée to a large pan. Mix and season with salt and pepper (to taste). Simmer for 10 minutes.

06 Blitz with a handheld food processor. Enjoy!

PETITS POIS &
ROASTED GARLIC

INGREDIENTS

garlic
1 brown onion
thyme
500-g (1 lb 2-oz) packet of
frozen petits pois
vegetable stock (bouillon) cube
cider vinegar
fresh parsley
olive oil
salt and pepper

01 Preheat your oven to 200°C fan (220°C/450°F/Gas Mark 8).

02 Cut the top off the garlic bulb, wrap in tin foil, pour a generous amount of olive oil over then close the tin foil. Bake for 45 minutes until soft and mellow.

03 Chop up an onion and add the leaves from 3 thyme sprigs. Fry in a little oil until soft.

04 Add the frozen petits pois, a stock cube, 1 litre (4 cups) of boiling water, 2 tablespoons of cider vinegar and salt and pepper. Wait until it boils and then reduce the heat to low, add 2 handfuls of fresh parsley and leave to simmer for 10 minutes.

05 Squeeze the cloves out from the roasted garlic and into the pan. Take a handheld blender and blitz the soup until smooth. Enjoy!

CURRIED CAULIFLOWER

INGREDIENTS

1 cauliflower
2 brown onions
garlic
ground coriander
ground turmeric
ground cumin
400-g (14-oz) tin of
coconut milk
vegetable stock (bouillon) cube
cashews
1 red chilli
lime
olive oil
salt and pepper

01 Chop a cauliflower, 2 onions and 3 garlic cloves up roughly. Heat some oil in a pan. Add the onions to the pan and fry until soft and translucent. Add garlic, ½ teaspoon of ground coriander, ½ teaspoon of turmeric, 1 teaspoon of cumin and fry for 1–2 minutes to release the aromas. Season with salt and pepper.

02 Add the curried cauliflower, coconut milk, stock cube and 1 litre (4 cups) of water. Stir well and bring to the boil. Once boiling, turn the heat down to low and simmer for 20 minutes (or until the cauliflower is tender and soft).

03 Blitz with a handheld food processor until smooth. Season with salt and pepper again.

04 Toast some cashews in a pan for a few minutes. De-seed and slice a chilli.

05 Serve the soup with the toasted cashews, a few slices of red chilli and a squeeze of lime.

INGREDIENTS

cumin seeds
mustard seeds
2 red chillies
2 onions
garlic
fresh ginger
2 x 400-g (14-oz) tins of green
jackfruit pieces
400 g (2¼ cups) rice
ground coriander
ground turmeric
tomato purée (paste)
500-ml (17-oz) jar of passata
(strained tomatoes)
coconut cream
olive oil

**THE MEATIEST VEGAN
CURRY YOU'LL EVER
MUNCH. SIMPLE AS THAT.**

MIGHTY JACKFRUIT CURRY [VG]

01 Add a glug of oil to a frying pan (skillet) and add 1 teaspoon cumin seeds and the same of mustard seeds, pan-frying for a minute to release the aroma. Add 2 chopped red chillies, 2 chopped onions, 5 chopped garlic cloves and a chopped 2.5-cm (1-inch) piece of ginger. Cook until the onions are soft and translucent.

02 Drain and rinse your jackfruit (to remove as much salt as possible).

03 Get the rice on and cook according to the instructions on the packet.

04 Add 1½ teaspoons ground coriander, 1 teaspoon turmeric, 2 tablespoons tomato purée and the jackfruit. Mix together, pour in the passata, cover your pan and cook for 10 minutes.

05 Uncover and shred the jackfruit a bit and allow the sauce to thicken. Add 2 tablespoons coconut cream and a little water if necessary. Mix everything together.

06 Bubble the curry down until it is nice and thick. Serve on a bed of steaming rice.

INGREDIENTS

2 brown onions
garlic
1 carrot
1 cauliflower
cinnamon stick
cardamom pods
cumin seeds
bay leaves
ground turmeric
basmati rice
vegan margarine
vegetable oil
salt and pepper

FRAGRANT VEGGIE PILAF [VG]

01 Finely chop 2 brown onions and 2 garlic cloves then fry them over a low heat with a glug of oil until the onions are soft and translucent.

02 Chop a carrot into small cubes. Break up the cauliflower into little florets and chop up finely. Add to the pan and fry for 2 minutes.

03 Add your spices – 1 cinnamon stick, 2 crushed cardamom pods, 1 teaspoon of cumin seeds, 3 bay leaves and 1 teaspoon of turmeric. Season with salt and pepper. Stir well.

04 Meanwhile, rinse 300 g (1¾ cups) basmati rice and add to the pan with 700 ml (3 cups) water. Mix well then cook on low for 20 minutes or so until the rice is cooked and there is no liquid left in the pan.

05 Fluff up your rice, remove the cinnamon stick and bay leaves, and add a heaped tablespoon of margarine before serving.

AHHHHH PILAF. THOSE AROMATIC SMELLS. THE BEAUTY OF THIS RECIPE IS THAT IT IS ALL IN ONE POT. YOU CAN ADD WHATEVER VEG YOU LIKE TO IT SO IF YOU'VE GOT ANY LEFTOVER PRODUCE, CHUCK IT IN!

INGREDIENTS

1 aubergine (eggplant)

1 butternut squash

1 brown onion

fresh ginger

garlic

sesame oil

garam masala

chilli (hot red pepper) flakes

tomato purée (paste)

400 g (2¼ cups) basmati rice

350-g (12½-oz) pot of dairy-free yogurt (we use The Coconut Collaborative)

fresh coriander (cilantro)

cashew nuts

1 lime

olive oil

salt and pepper

CREAMY, COCONUTTY, SOOTHING. WHAT MORE COULD YOU WANT FROM A CURRY? THE CASHEWS BRING THE CRUNCH.

CREAMY VEGAN KORMA [★] [VG]

01 Preheat your oven to 180°C fan (200°C/400°F/Gas Mark 6).

02 Cube 1 aubergine and 1 butternut squash. Add to a baking tray. Drizzle with olive oil, season with salt and pepper and place in the preheated oven for 35 minutes.

03 Meanwhile, get your korma on. Finely chop 1 brown onion and grate a piece of ginger and 2 garlic cloves. Heat a large frying pan (skillet) with 1½ tablespoons of sesame oil and add the onion, ginger and garlic. Fry until soft, and then add 2 teaspoons of garam masala, a teaspoon of chilli flakes and 2 tablespoons of tomato purée. Stir everything together, and then add 200 ml (¾ cup plus 1 tablespoon) of water.

04 Get basmati rice in a pan with 2 parts boiling water. Cook until the water has been absorbed.

05 Add the 'yogurt' to the korma and stir it in. Add your roasted vegetables, with a large handful of chopped coriander (reserve some to garnish), 60 g (½ cup) cashew nuts and the juice of a lime.

06 Serve the korma over the steaming hot rice with the remaining coriander leaves scattered on top.

INGREDIENTS

2 white onions
3 large leeks
arborio rice
single-serve bottle of white
wine (187 ml/6 fl oz)
1 vegetarian stock (bouillon)
cube
pecorino
veggie Parmesan
olive oil
salt and pepper

THE DUTTIEST LITTLE
RIZZY THIS SIDE OF THE
ATLANTIC. MAKE SURE
YOU COOK THE LEEKS
UNTIL THEY ARE SILKY
AND SMOOTH – LOW AND
SLOW PAPI.

SILKY LEEK RISOTTO

01 Dice up your onions and leeks.

02 Heat a frying pan (skillet) with a glug of olive oil over a medium heat. Add your onions and leeks, cooking until they are soft and translucent. Season with salt and pepper.

03 Take one-quarter of the mixture out, put to the side and salt generously.

04 Pour in 300 g (1½ cups) risotto rice. Mix for a minute, so that the rice becomes slightly translucent.

05 Wine time! Pour in the bottle of white wine and mix while it slowly evaporates.

06 Mix your veggie stock cubes with boiling water.

07 Ladle in the stock, mix the risotto and then wait until the risotto dries up.

08 Once it has dried up, add another ladle. Repeat until the rice is al dente. Keep ladling in the stock if need be.

09 Add half a grated block of pecorino and half a grated block of veggie parmesan, and mix thoroughly.

10 Take the pan off the heat and serve with some of the remaining salted leek and onion mixture on top!

INGREDIENTS

2 butternut squash
vegetable stock (bouillon) cube
garlic
orzo pasta
fresh basil
goat's cheese
veggie Parmesan
olive oil
salt and pepper

THE OOZIEST ORZO ABOUT
– THE PERFECT AUTUMN
WARMER. THE BASIL AND
THE GOAT'S CHEESE
REALLY FRESHEN THE DISH
UP SO DON'T SKIP EITHER
OF THEM. ALSO, WHEN
YOU FIRST ROAST YOUR
BUTTERNUT SQUASH, YOU
DON'T WANT IT TO GET
BROWN AND CHARRED.
JUST SOFT. SO KEEP AN
EYE ON IT.

OOZY BUTTERNUT ORZO [★]

01 Preheat your oven to 180°C fan (200°C/400°F/Gas Mark 6).

02 Cut 2 butternut squash into cubes, and place in a baking tray. Drizzle with olive oil and season with salt and pepper. Place in the preheated oven for 30 minutes or until soft.

03 Remove the squash when it's soft. Place three-quarters in a blender. Place the remainder back in the oven until brown and caramelized.

04 Add a vegetable stock cube and 550 ml (2¼ cups) water into a blender. Blitz. You want quite a loose purée consistency.

05 Get a large frying pan (skillet) over the heat. Add 1 clove of chopped garlic with a splash of olive oil. Once softened, pour in the squash purée. Mix it about, and then add 500 g (3 scant cups) orzo.

06 Keep beating the orzo about, and pouring in splashes of water until the orzo has cooked through and resembles a loose, oozy risotto. At this point, add your remaining squash, and a handful of chopped basil (leave some whole leaves to garnish). Mix it all together and turn off the heat.

07 Add large dollops of goat's cheese onto the orzo, sprinkle over some veggie Parmesan, scatter on some whole basil leaves and serve with a last drizzle of olive oil! Enjoy!

INGREDIENTS

2 brown onions
garlic
ground cumin
ground cinnamon
harissa
3 aubergines (eggplants)
400-g (14-oz) tin of tomatoes
400-g (14-oz) tin of chickpeas
couscous
1 lemon
pitted dates
coriander (cilantro)
salt and pepper

A DELICIOUS VEGAN
TAGINE. SLOW COOKING
IS THE KEY HERE. MAKE
SURE YOU ADD THE SPICES
AT THE START SO THEY
RELEASE THEIR OILS. BIG
UP THE TAGINE.

CHICKPEA, AUBERGINE & DATE TAGINE [VG]

01 Chop 2 brown onions roughly, and finely chop 2 garlic cloves. Place a large frying pan (skillet) over a medium heat and add a little oil. Add your spices (1½ teaspoons of ground cumin, 1 teaspoon of ground cinnamon and 3 teaspoons of harissa) and cook until the onions start to look translucent.

02 Chop 3 aubergines into large chunks and add to the pan. Keep cooking for another 10 minutes, stirring continuously to get all the spices and flavours into the aubergine.

03 Next, add the tomatoes, chickpeas and their water. Season with salt and pepper, give it a good stir, then place the lid on for 1 hour, or until thick and the aubergine is cooked through.

04 With a few minutes to go, cook 400 g (14 oz) couscous according to the packet instructions, then add a squeeze of lemon juice.

05 Stir a handful of pitted dates into the tagine. Serve the tagine on top of couscous and garnish with a squeeze of lemon and a scattering of coriander leaves.

INGREDIENTS

1 cauliflower
ground cumin
ground coriander
ground turmeric
garlic
1 lemon
400-g (14-oz) pot of
coconut yogurt
1 cucumber
200 g (7 oz) pomegranate
seeds
400 g (2⅓ cups) couscous
raisins
fresh mint
fresh parsley
olive oil
salt and pepper

**A REAL VEGGIE
SHOWSTOPPER. THE
CAULIFLOWER IS SO
MOREISH. TRY AND FIND
A NICE BIG CAULIFLOWER
FOR THIS – PEOPLE ARE
GOING TO BE FIGHTING
OVER IT.**

BAKED SPICED CAULIFLOWER WITH TZATZIKI [VG]

01 Preheat your oven to 200°C fan (220°C/450°F/Gas Mark 8).

02 Trim the base of a large cauliflower and remove any green leaves.

03 In a bowl, combine 2 teaspoons of ground cumin, 1 teaspoon of ground coriander and ½ teaspoon of turmeric. Add a crushed garlic clove and salt and pepper. Pour in 2 tablespoons of olive oil. Mix together well until you have a thick paste.

04 Spread the marinade over the cauliflower and place on a lined baking tray and roast until the surface is dry – around 45 minutes.

05 Meanwhile, it's tzatziki time. Zest 1 lemon and squeeze its juices into a bowl with half the pot of coconut yogurt.

06 Finely grate a cucumber (squeeze the gratings to remove excess moisture) and add to the yogurt with a handful of chopped mint and 100 g (3½ oz) pomegranate seeds. Season with salt and pepper and set aside.

07 Couscous time. Add the cous cous to a bowl. Cover with boiling water so there is about 2.5 cm (1 inch) of water on top of the cous cous. Allow it to absorb the water for 5 minutes, and then fluff if up with a fork. Add 150 g (1 cup) raisins, a handful of chopped parsley, another 100 g (3½ oz) pomegranate seeds, salt, pepper and olive oil. Mix together.

08 When cooked, let the cauliflower cool and serve in thick slices with a spoonful of your homemade tzatziki and a sprinkling of fresh pomegranate seeds, on top of your cous cous. Garnish with torn mint and parsley.

5

FLASHY MOB

CAPONATA PARMIGIANA

SERVES 4
2 hrs

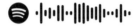

St. Germain
Rose Rouge

INGREDIENTS

3 large aubergines (eggplants)
plain (all-purpose) flour
1 red onion
fresh parsley
capers
pitted Kalamata olives
red wine vinegar
3 x 400-g (14-oz) tins of plum
tomatoes
3 large mozzarella balls
veggie Parmesan
olive oil
salt and pepper

**A TWIST ON AN ITALIAN
CLASSIC THAT IS EVEN
BETTER COLD THE NEXT
DAY. DON'T FORGET TO
SALT YOUR AUBERGINES
TO REMOVE THE BITTER
TASTE AND DRAW OUT
EXCESS WATER.**

01 Preheat your oven to 160°C fan (180°C/360°F/Gas Mark 4).

02 Cut the aubergines lengthwise into ½–1-cm (¼–½-inch) strips. Place them in a bowl and sprinkle generously with sea salt. After half an hour, pour the excess water out of the bowls. Coat the aubergine slices with flour.

03 Pour some oil into a frying pan (skillet) over medium heat and fry the aubergines until lightly browned on each side. Remove from the pan and set aside.

04 Chop the onion and sauté in the pan with some more olive oil, if necessary. Allow the onion to soften until translucent and then add a handful of chopped parsley stalks, 2 tablespoons each of capers and olives with 4 tablespoons of red wine vinegar. Stir well and, once the vinegar has evaporated, add the tomatoes. Break them up and leave the sauce to simmer for 6–7 minutes, until very thick. Add some chopped parsley leaves, then season with salt and pepper and remove from the heat.

05 Spoon some of the sauce into an oven dish. Layer up with aubergine, tomato sauce and sliced mozzarella. Keep repeating until the dish is full. Finish off with a layer of mozzarella and grated Parmesan. Drizzle over some olive oil and season with salt and pepper.

06 Place the dish in the oven and leave for 35 minutes, then place it under the grill (broiler) until the cheese is golden and bubbling.

07 Leave for at least 30 minutes to set. Then slice up the parmigiana and tuck in!

INGREDIENTS

4 aubergines (eggplants)
red miso
maple syrup
mirin
400 g (2¼ cups) jasmine rice
toasted sesame oil
sesame seeds

**MAKE SURE YOU
FOLLOW THE SOAKING
INSTRUCTIONS IN THIS
RECIPE – IT IS KEY TO
MAKE SURE YOU GET THE
SWEETEST, SQUIDGIEST
AUBERGINE.**

MISO-GLAZED STICKY AUBERGINES WITH SESAME RICE [VG]

01 Preheat your oven to 230°C fan (250°C/480°F/Gas Mark 9).

02 Peel and cut 4 aubergines, about 2–3-cm (1-inch) thick wedges. Soak in water for 5–10 minutes to remove tannins (which make aubergines taste bitter). The water you pour out will be brown.

03 Make the sauce by mixing 150 g (5½ oz) miso, 150 g (5½ oz) honey and 75 g (2½ oz) mirin in a bowl. Set aside.

04 Coat the bottom of an oven dish in oil. Pat the aubergines dry with paper towels and place in the oven dish. Arrange so that there are no overlaps and place the dish in the oven.

05 Meanwhile, cook the jasmine rice according to the packet instructions. Add a teaspoon of sesame oil to the cooked rice.

06 Once the aubergines are nearly done (check if a fork can go in easily), add most of the sauce and place back in the oven. Make sure the sauce doesn't burn! Once almost ready, brush with any leftover sauce for added stickiness.

07 Serve on a bed of rice with sesame seeds scattered on top.

SERVES 4
1 hr

The Haggis Horns
Way of the Haggis

INGREDIENTS

vegetable stock (bouillon) cube
500 g (3¼ cups) polenta (fine cornmeal)
6 portobello mushrooms
1 red onion
garlic
balsamic vinegar
butter
veggie Parmesan
fresh parsley
olive oil

IF I HAD A POUND FOR EVERY TIME I'D BEEN TOLD THAT POLENTA IS BORING I'D BE A MILLIONAIRE. WELL, THIS IS THE DISH TO PROVE THE POLENTA HATERS WRONG. RICH. CREAMY. CHEESY. IT HAS IT ALL.

CREAMY POLENTA WITH PORTOBELLO MUSHROOMS

01 Add the stock cube to 2 litres (8 cups) water in a pan, bring to the boil, add polenta and whisk to prevent lumps. Cook according to the packet instructions.

02 Reduce the heat to medium-low so the polenta bubbles (but doesn't go everywhere), making sure to stir every few minutes so it doesn't catch or burn. Cook for about 30 minutes until it thickens.

03 Meanwhile, slice up your mushrooms, chop up the onion and dice 2 garlic cloves.

04 Heat a frying pan (skillet) with some olive oil, add the onion and when it starts to look translucent, add the garlic. When both are soft, add your mushrooms and a splash of balsamic vinegar.

05 When the polenta is cooked, add a big knob (pat) of butter and a handful of cheese, and mix well so that it all melts.

06 Back to the mushrooms. When the balsamic is slightly sticky and the mushrooms are plump and soft, serve the mushrooms on top of the creamy polenta. Garnish with chopped parsley.

INGREDIENTS

cashews
400 g (2¼ cups) basmati rice
1 brown onion
ginger
garlic
chilli powder
garam masala
ground turmeric
200 g (7 oz) tomato purée
(paste)
200-g (7-oz) packet of paneer
double (heavy) cream
spinach
fresh coriander (cilantro)
olive oil
salt and pepper

A PUNJABI SPECIAL FOR UNDER A TENNER. SACK OFF THE TAKEAWAY AND WHIP UP THIS INSTEAD. ONE NOTE OF CAUTION: BE CAREFUL WHEN HANDLING THE TURMERIC, IT STAINS EVERYTHING!

SHAHI SPINACH PANEER

01 Soak a handful of cashews in warm water for at least 15 minutes whilst preparing the other ingredients.

02 Get the rice on by following the instructions on the packet.

03 Meanwhile, dice a brown onion. Peel a 2.5-cm (1-inch) piece of ginger and dice. Peel and cut up 4 garlic cloves. Place it all into a frying pan (skillet) with a drizzle of oil and sauté. Add salt, black pepper, ½ teaspoon of red chilli powder, ½ teaspoon of garam masala and ½ a teaspoon of turmeric.

04 Let simmer until the onion gets soft and translucent. Turn off the stove and let it cool slightly.

05 After the cashews have been soaked and onions cooked, add them both to a blender to make a smooth paste.

06 Heat some olive oil in a frying pan, then add the paste. Cook on low until most of the moisture evaporates, then add the tomato purée.

07 Stir well and cook until the oil starts to ooze out from the sides. Stir frequently to make sure that it is not sticking to the bottom of the pan.

08 Add ½ teaspoon of garam masala and mix well. Cube the paneer, add to the pan, mix well and allow to simmer for 2 minutes.

09 Add 4 tablespoons of double cream and mix in. Add the spinach and let cook for a few more minutes.

10 Serve on a bed of rice and garnish with fresh coriander leaves.

SERVES 4
2 hrs

Natty Reeves
Solace

INGREDIENTS

1 large butternut squash
2 sweet potatoes
2 red (bell) peppers
1 brown onion
garlic
400g (14oz) spinach
200g (7oz) feta
1 lemon

SQUASH, SPINACH & RED PEPPER PIE

01   Preheat your oven to 160°C fan (180°C/360°F/Gas Mark 4).

02   Peel the squash and sweet potatoes and cut into cubes. Put in an oven dish, season with salt and pepper and drizzle with olive oil. Cook for 50 minutes, or until cooked through.

03   At the same time, put the whole red peppers on a baking tray and roast in the oven for 40 minutes.

04   Meanwhile, finely chop the onion and 2 cloves of garlic. Add to a frying pan (skillet) with a splash of olive oil. Fry until the onions are soft, then add your spinach. Wilt the spinach down and season with salt and pepper.

05   Transfer the spinach mixture to a sieve. Squeeze with a wooden spoon to get rid of excess moisture. Add the spinach to a mixing bowl and crumble in half of the feta and the zest of the lemon.

250g (9oz) ricotta
4 eggs
250g (9oz) filo (phyllo) pastry
sesame seeds
olive oil
salt and pepper

THIS BANGING VEGGIE PIE IS WARMING, FILLING & THE SESAME SEEDS PERFECT THE CRUNCHY TOP!

06   Remove the red peppers from the oven, put them in a bowl, cover with clingfilm (plastic wrap) and leave to cool. Peel off the skins, remove the seeds and cut into quarters.

07   Remove the potatoes and squash from the oven and roughly mash together in a mixing bowl. Add the remaining feta, ricotta, and 4 eggs. Season with salt and pepper, and mix everything together. Keep the oven on.

08   Pie time. Brush a 900-g (2-lb) loaf tin or other pie dish with olive oil. Add a layer of filo pastry. Brush with olive oil. Then repeat with 4 more layers of filo.

09   Put the spinach mixture on the bottom, followed by the potato and squash mixture. Top it with the roasted red peppers and fold the edges of the pastry over the top. Add 3–4 crumpled sheets of filo on the top for extra crunch. Brush well with olive oil and sprinkle with sesame seeds.

10   Bake the pie in the still-warm oven for 50 minutes, or until golden brown.

11   Slice the pie and tuck in!

THE N'CASCIATA

SERVES 4
1 hr

 ·||II··|·||||·||||·||·

Franc Moody
Dopamine

INGREDIENTS

5 aubergines (eggplants)
1 red onion
garlic
fresh parsley
capers
red wine vinegar
pitted Kalamata olives
400-g (14-oz) tin of
plum tomatoes
500 g (1 lb 2 oz) dried rigatoni
pasta
veggie Parmesan
olive oil

A SERIOUSLY IMPRESSIVE
DISH. AN AUBERGINE AND
PASTA CAKE, BASICALLY
YOU CAN USE A CIRCULAR
CAKE TIN OR A SQUARE
BAKING DISH. JUST MAKE
SURE THE SIDES ARE
HIGH ENOUGH.

01 Preheat your oven to 180°C fan (200°C/400°F/Gas Mark 6).

02 Cut 3 aubergines into long, thin slices. Grill (broil) each slice (DON'T ADD OIL!) on a griddle (ridged stovetop) pan until charred and soft. If you don't have a griddle, use a frying pan (skillet). Set the aubergine slices to one side.

03 Time to make the sauce! Chop another 2 aubergines into 2-cm (¾-inch) chunks. Dice a red onion and grate the garlic.

04 Add the diced aubergine to a frying pan, but again, don't add any oil. Cook until the aubergine is evenly browned.

05 At this point, add a glug of olive oil, the diced onion, grated garlic and a large handful of chopped parsley and cook for another couple of minutes.

06 Add 2 tablespoons capers, 3 tablespoons red wine vinegar and a handful of pitted Kalamata olives to the pan and cook for another minute.

07 Add the plum tomatoes and crush with a wooden spoon. Simmer for 10 minutes.

08 While the sauce is simmering away, boil the rigatoni until al dente and add it to the sauce with a splash of the pasta water. Stir to combine.

09 Find a deep, ovenproof dish (preferably metal). Line it with most of your sliced aubergines. First line the bottom, making sure all the sides overlap. Then place them around the edges until all sides are covered.

10 Spoon in your rigatoni, and then place the remaining aubergine slices over the top so it is covered. Grate over some Parmesan, and then cover with tin foil. Bake in the preheated oven for 20 minutes.

11 Remove the dish from the oven and take off the tin foil. Place the dish back in the oven for 4 minutes so the Parmesan melts. Remove from the oven.

12 Place a plate on top of the dish. Flip it, then ease the tin off the pasta cake. Slice it up and tuck in!

LEAVE THE DISH TO SET FOR 30 MINUTES SO THAT IT'S EASY TO SERVE UP! BAKING THE AUBERGINE SLICES BEFOREHAND ENSURES THEY ARE NICE AND SOFT. THIS ONE IS AN ABSOLUTE BELTER SERVED COLD THE NEXT DAY.

VEGGIE MOUSSAKA

01   Preheat your oven to 180°C fan (200°C/400°F/Gas Mark 6).

02   Finely slice the aubergines lengthways. Place on a rack, cover in salt and pepper, then bake for 15 minutes.

03   Meanwhile, in a bowl, add a crumbled block of feta, the ricotta, the zest of a lemon and an egg, and season with salt, pepper and olive oil. Mix everything together and set aside for later.

04   Finely chop your onions and 2 garlic cloves. Fry in a large saucepan until soft, then add 1 teaspoon of cinnamon and 2 teaspoons of dried oregano. Season with salt and pepper, and then add a large handful of chopped parsley.

05   Mix together, and then add your tinned tomatoes and 600 ml (2½ cups) water.

06   Wash 350 g (2 cups) red lentils, then pour them into the sauce. Mix, and then cook over a medium heat for 15–20 minutes until the lentils have cooked through and the sauce has thickened. Remove from the heat.

07   Layering time. Into a baking dish, spoon in half your lentil mixture. Then cover it with half your cooked aubergine slices. Cover the aubergine with the other half of the lentil mix, and then cover this with your remaining aubergines. Cover it all with your feta and ricotta mix, then place under a hot grill (broiler) for 10 minutes, or until the feta and ricotta mix starts to get little burnt marks over it.

08   Remove from the oven, let rest for 30 minutes, then slice up and enjoy!

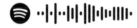
INGREDIENTS

1 red (bell) pepper
1 small butternut squash
2 sweet potatoes
400 g (2¼ cups) basmati rice
2 red onions
garlic
tomato purée (paste)
1 red chilli
fresh parsley
paprika
400-g (14-oz) tin of black beans
2 x 400-g (14-oz) tins of tomatoes
dark (bittersweet) chocolate
brown sugar
lemon
olive oil
salt and pepper

ROASTED VEGETABLE FEIJOADA [VG]

01 Preheat your oven to 180°C fan (200°C/400°F/Gas Mark 6).

02 Chop up the red pepper, butternut squash and sweet potatoes. Add to a baking tray and roast in the oven for 40 minutes.

03 Cook the rice according to the instructions on the packet.

04 Dice the red onions and 2 garlic cloves. Gently fry the onion, garlic, 1 tablespoon tomato purée and the chopped red chilli (de-seeded) with a little olive oil for 5 minutes. Chop the parsley stalks and add with 1 teaspoon paprika and fry for another minute. Season generously with salt and pepper.

05 Drain your beans then add them to the mix along with the tomatoes. Add 60 g (2 oz) of dark chocolate and a heaped tablespoon of brown sugar. Mix well and allow to simmer and bubble down.

06 Add the roasted veg to the mix. Stir them in and cook for another 10 minutes so the vegetables absorb all the flavour.

07 Serve on rice, squeeze lots of lemon juice on top and add the rest of the parsley for garnish.

A BRAZILIAN CLASSIC WITH A VEGGIE TWIST. ADDING CHOCOLATE BRINGS THE RICHNESS HERE AND THERE SHOULD BE SOME LEFTOVER FOR NIBBLING AT THE END.

INGREDIENTS

1 brown onion
garlic
sugar
2 x 400-g (14-oz) tins of
chopped tomatoes
Kalamata olives
4 fennel heads
dried breadcrumbs
200-g (7-oz) packet of taleggio
olive oil
salt and pepper

THE FENNEL BECOMES ALL UNCTUOUS WHEN YOU SLOW COOK IT. MAKE SURE THE BREADCRUMBS ARE GOLDEN AND CRUNCHY BEFORE SERVING.

FENNEL & TOMATO BAKE WITH TALEGGIO & BREADCRUMB TOPPING

01 Preheat your oven to 160°C fan (180°C/360°F/Gas Mark 4).

02 Chop an onion and 3 garlic cloves finely and fry with a glug of oil until the onion is soft and translucent. Add 2 teaspoons of sugar. Once it has dissolved, add your tomatoes and allow to cook over a low heat for 20 minutes so that it bubbles down into a lovely rich sauce.

03 Take the sauce off the heat. Chop a handful of Kalamata olives in half and add to the sauce.

04 Heat some olive oil in another saucepan. Meanwhile, chop 4 fennel heads into large chunks, add to the saucepan, cover and stew over a low heat for 15 minutes. Add your tomato sauce and season with salt and pepper. Simmer until the sauce is thick. Pour into an oven dish.

05 Top the dish with the breadcrumbs, drizzle generously with olive oil and crumble over the taleggio. Bake for 20 minutes until the breadcrumbs and cheese are golden.

06 Remove from the oven, spoon it out onto plates and enjoy!

INGREDIENTS

4 sweet potatoes

300 g (10½ oz) quinoa

200 g (7 oz) kale

lemon

tahini

honey

chipotle chilli paste

flaked (slivered) almonds

pomegranate seeds

olive oil

salt and pepper

A GREAT SUMMER DISH – THE SWEET POTATOES COOK PERFECTLY IN THE COALS OF THE BBQ. THE TAHINI DRESSING IS SO CREAMY, YOU WON'T BELIEVE ITS VEGAN.

LOADED BBQ SWEET POTATOES WITH TAHINI DRESSING

01 Set up the BBQ and fire up the BBQ coals.

02 Wash 4 sweet potatoes, rub with a little olive oil and salt, then double wrap in tin foil. When the coals are glowing red, put the wrapped potatoes directly on top of them for 15 minutes, turn, and cook for another 15 minutes.

03 While these are cooking, put a pot of water on to boil. When bubbling, add the quinoa. Cook for 15 minutes.

04 De-stem the kale leaves and thinly chop. Add to a large bowl, add some olive oil and massage the leaves for a minute (it makes them more tender).

05 Add the juice of a lemon, 2 tablespoons of tahini, a generous tablespoon of honey and 2 tablespoons of chipotle paste into the bowl. Season with salt and pepper, then mix thoroughly.

06 Remove a potato and check if it's cooked thoroughly. Take the quinoa off the heat, drain and toss with your kale and tahini. Split the potatoes open and layer with dressed quinoa and then kale on top.

07 Quickly toast the flaked almonds in a frying pan (skillet), then top the potatoes with them. Shake a handful of pomegranate seeds on top. Enjoy!

FAKEAWAY
MOB

6

INGREDIENTS

3 red onions
cumin seeds
garam masala
ground coriander
fresh ginger
fresh coriander (coriander)
baking powder
chickpea (gram) flour
150-g/5½-oz pot of
coconut yogurt
1 cucumber
fresh mint
4 brioche buns
mango chutney
vegetable oil
salt and pepper

**THESE BHAJI BURGERS
ARE THE ONE. THE FRESH
HOMEMADE COCONUT
RAITA MAKES THEM!
SWITCH OUT THE BRIOCHE
BUNS FOR A NORMAL
SEEDED BAP TO KEEP IT
SUITABLE FOR THE VEEGS!**

BIG BOY BHAJI BURGERS [★]

01 Finely slice 3 red onions. Add them to a bowl with 2 teaspoons cumin seeds, 2 teaspoons garam masala and 2 teaspoons ground coriander. Add a teaspoon of grated ginger, a tablespoon of chopped coriander stalks, a teaspoon of baking powder, 4 tablespoons chickpea flour and 6 tablespoons water. Mix everything together until it resembles a chunky, oniony batter.

02 Make your raita. Add the coconut yogurt to a bowl. Add a large handful of grated cucumber (squeeze the gratings to get rid of excess water), a handful of chopped mint and coriander leaves, and salt and pepper. Mix well.

03 Heat some vegetable oil in a frying pan (skillet). Add a tablespoon of your bhaji batter. Flatten it out and fry for 2–3 minutes on each side until golden brown. Cook 2 bhajis per burger.

04 Cut 4 brioche buns in half and whack them under the grill (broiler) to toast up.

05 Assembly time. Add a big dollop of raita to the bap. Then add a bhaji. Then more raita, then another bhaji. Top with a big dollop of mango chutney and some mint leaves. Take a big bite and enjoy!

INGREDIENTS

1 cauliflower
1 broccoli
plain (all-purpose) flour
2 eggs
dried breadcrumbs
1 cucumber
200-g (7-oz) bag of radishes
1 lime
3 gem lettuces
fresh coriander (cilantro)
mayonnaise
sriracha
1 avocado
olive oil
salt and pepper

YOU WANT THE BROCCOLI AND THE CAULIFLOWER FLORETS TO BE PERFECT BITE-SIZED PIECES SO BEAR THAT IN MIND WHILE PREPPING! LEAVE THE CAULIFLOWER IN THE OVEN UNTIL PERFECTLY BROWN AND CRUNCHY.

BANG BANG CAULIFLOWER SALAD BOWLS

01 Preheat your oven to 160°C fan (180°C/360°F/Gas Mark 4).

02 Break the cauliflower and broccoli into florets.

03 Get 3 bowls out. Add some flour to one, 2 beaten eggs to another and breadcrumbs to the last.

04 Dip the broccoli and cauliflower florets into the flour, the eggs and the breadcrumbs, in that order. Add baking paper to a baking tray. Season the veg with salt and drizzle with olive oil, and then put the tray in the oven for 30 minutes until golden and crunchy.

05 Finely chop a cucumber and the radishes. Add to a bowl with the juice of half a lime, the chopped gem lettuces, 3 tablespoons of olive oil, a handful of coriander, and salt and pepper. Mix together and set aside.

06 Into a bowl add 6 tablespoons of mayo, 2 tablespoons of sriracha and the juice of half a lime. Mix everything together.

07 Serving time. Add the zingy radish salad to a bowl. Top with bang bang veg, some avocado slices, a big dollop of sriracha mayo and some fresh coriander leaves. Enjoy!

BLACK PEPPER TOFU [★]

INGREDIENTS

2 x 280-g (10-oz) packets of
tofu (we use The Tofoo Co.
Naked Tofu)
cornflour (cornstarch)
400 g (2 cups) basmati rice
butter
1 white onion
garlic
fresh ginger
crushed black peppercorns
white sugar
light soy sauce
dark soy sauce
1 red chilli
4 spring onions (scallions)
vegetable oil

01 Chop the tofu into cubes. Coat in cornflour.

02 Add some vegetable oil to a wok. Fry the tofu until browned and remove from the wok.

03 Get the rice on (follow the instructions on the packet).

04 Clean the wok and place over a medium heat. Add a splash of oil. Add 4 tablespoons of butter, along with the chopped onion, finely chopped garlic and a large piece of fresh ginger. Fry until everything is soft. At this point, add 2 tablespoons crushed black peppercorns and 2 tablespoons white sugar. Stir them in. Once the sugar has dissolved, add 5 tablespoons each of light and dark soy sauce.

05 Stir it all together, and then add a chopped red chilli and 3 chopped spring onions. Stir, and then re-add your tofu. Stir it in, add another tablespoon of butter, allowing it to melt, then remove the tofu from the heat.

06 Serve the tofu on top of a mound of steaming rice, garnish with another chopped spring onion and enjoy!

SUCH A DELICIOUS DISH.
AND A GREAT WAY TO
USE UP ANY LEFTOVER
BLACK PEPPER! TASTE
THE TOFU AT THE END. IF
IT'S TOO SUGARY, ADD A
BIT MORE PEPPER. IF IT'S
TOO PEPPERY, ADD A BIT
MORE SUGAR. GET THAT
BALANCE RIGHT.

QUESADILLAS (3 WAYS)

SERVES 4
15 mins

An Der Beat
Knuf!

MAKE IT VEGAN BY SUBSTITUTING THE CREAM CHEESE FOR A VEGAN CREAM CHEESE ALTERNATIVE!

SPINACH & ARTICHOKE QUESADILLAS

INGREDIENTS

garlic
marinated artichoke hearts
baby spinach
cream cheese
8 large flour tortillas
olive oil

01 Heat some olive oil in a frying pan (skillet). Chop up 2 garlic cloves and add to the pan, sautéing for 1 minute.

02 Cut up the artichoke hearts and add to the pan along with 3 large handfuls of the baby spinach. Stir to combine and cook until the spinach begins to wilt.

03 Add the cream cheese and salt and pepper to the pan, and stir to combine. Heat all the way through and then put to the side.

04 Place another non-stick pan on the stove over a medium–high heat. Put one tortilla in the pan and fill with one-quarter of the mixture and half a handful of baby spinach – spread only on one half of the tortilla.

05 Fold in half, cook until the bottom is brown (around 2 minutes) and flip to brown the other side.

06 Repeat for the remaining tortillas.

07 Slice and serve!

CHEESY CORN & SMASHED AVOCADO QUESADILLAS

INGREDIENTS

garlic
325-g (11½-oz) tin of corn
2 avocados
Cheddar
8 large flour tortillas

01 Dice 5 garlic cloves and pan-fry until soft.

02 Drain the tin of corn and set to the side.

03 Cut, de-stone and then smash the avocados.

04 Grate your Cheddar.

05 Place a non-stick frying pan on the stove over a medium–high heat. Put one tortilla in the pan and fill with some cooked garlic, smashed avocado and some corn – spread only on one half of the tortilla. Sprinkle over some grated cheese.

06 Fold in half, cook until the bottom is brown (around 2 minutes) and flip to brown the other side.

07 Repeat for the remaining tortillas. Slice and serve!

SWEET POTATO, BLACK BEAN & CARAMELIZED ONION QUESADILLAS [VG]

INGREDIENTS

3 red onions
2 sweet potatoes
balsamic vinegar
400-g (14-oz) tin of black beans
8 large flour tortillas
chilli (hot red pepper) flakes
olive oil

01 Slice the onions in long strips.

02 Put some oil in a frying pan over a medium heat until the oil is hot. Add the onions and some water. Cook for 30 minutes, stirring regularly until caramelized. Add water if the onions start sticking to the bottom of the pan or crisping.

03 Meanwhile, cook the sweet potatoes in a microwave or oven.

04 When the onions are caramelized, turn off the heat and add some balsamic vinegar, mixing it thoroughly.

05 Drain the tin of black beans and set aside.

06 Place a non-stick frying pan on the stove over a medium–high heat. Put one tortilla in the pan and fill with some sweet potato, black beans and caramelized onions – spread only on one half of the tortilla.

07 Fold in half, cook until the bottom is brown (around 2 minutes) and flip to brown the other side.

08 Repeat for the remaining tortillas. Slice and serve!

SERVES 4
40 mins

DJ Format
Behind The Scenes

INGREDIENTS

1 cauliflower
ground cumin
cayenne pepper
500 g (1 lb 2 oz) fresh peas (not frozen)
1 lemon
plain (all-purpose) flour
garlic
fresh mint
fresh coriander
1 pot of hummus
1 cucumber
3 tomatoes
1 romaine lettuce
vegetable oil
olive oil
salt and pepper

THESE LITTLE CRUNCHY PEA FALAFELS WILL BLOW YOUR MINDS. GREAT IN A SALAD. GREAT IN A PITTA. GREAT WHEREVER, REALLY. YOU CAN MAKE A CREAMY HUMMUS DRESSING BY JUST ADDING WATER, OLIVE OIL AND LEMON JUICE TO NORMAL HUMMUS. WHO KNEW!

CRUNCHY PEA FALAFEL SALAD [★]

01   Preheat oven to 180°C fan (200°C/400°F/Gas Mark 6).

02   Break a cauliflower up into little florets. Place them in a roasting tray. Add a teaspoon of cumin and a teaspoon of cayenne pepper. Drizzle over some olive oil, season with salt and pepper, and roast for 40 minutes.

03   Falafel time. Into a blender, add the peas, ½ teaspoon cayenne pepper, 1½ teaspoons ground cumin, the juice of ½ a lemon, a tablespoon of flour, a good grind of pepper, a pinch of salt, 2 grated garlic cloves, and a handful of both chopped mint and coriander (leave some of each to garnish). Blitz until you have a blended falafel mix. Take a small piece of the mixture and use your hands to form a ball that sticks together. If it doesn't, add a smidge more flour and blitz again.

04   Divide the mix into golfball-sized balls.

05   Heat 2 cm (¾ inch) of vegetable oil in a deep pan. To check it is hot enough, just put in a tiny bit of falafel mixture. When it starts bubbling, you are good to go. Carefully drop the falafels into the oil. Fry for 6–7 minutes, until brown and crunchy on the outside.

06   Set the falafels on some kitchen paper to absorb excess oil.

07   Get on your dressing. Into a bowl, add 2 heaped tablespoons of hummus, the juice of ½ a lemon and a glug of olive oil. Add a splash of water, season with salt and pepper, and mix with a fork. Keep adding water bit by bit until you have a smooth dressing consistency.

08   Sally time. Into a bowl, add a chopped cucumber (remove the seeds in the middle to make it less watery), 3 chopped tomatoes, a romaine lettuce, the cauliflower and the falafels. Add in the leftover mint and coriander leaves. Pour the dressing over the top, toss everything together and serve up!

INGREDIENTS

1 butternut squash (approx.
600 g/1 lb 5 oz)
2 carrots
1 brown onion
garlic
fresh ginger
garam masala
medium curry powder
ground cinnamon
mango chutney
500-ml (17-oz) jar of passata
(strained tomatoes)
plain yogurt
2 x 375-g (13-oz) puff pastry
sheets
1 egg
vegetable oil
salt and pepper

**THE FOOTBALL STADIUM
CLASSIC MADE VEGGIE.
BRUSH IT WITH EGG
YOLK TO MAKE SURE
THE PASTRY IS NICE AND
GOLDEN.**

VEGGIE BALTI PIE

01 Preheat your oven to 180°C fan (200°C/400°F/Gas Mark 6).

02 Roughly chop the butternut squash and carrots. Finely chop your onion, 2 cloves of garlic and a small piece of ginger.

03 Add the onion to a frying pan (skillet) with some oil and cook until soft. Add the other chopped veg. Then add 1 teaspoon of garam masala, 2 teaspoons of curry powder and 1 teaspoon of cinnamon. Mix it all in.

04 Add 2 teaspoons of mango chutney. Mix it in, and then add the passata. Stir it in, and reduce the curry down. Once it is thick, add 250 g/9 oz of plain yogurt. Season the balti with salt and pepper, then remove from the heat.

05 Roll out some puff pastry and lay it into a baking tray, Make sure it comes up and hangs over the sides. Lay some baking paper on top of it, and then pour in a bag of rice to weigh the pastry down. Add the tray to the oven for 12 minutes, then remove the baking paper and rice, and bake for another 3 minutes.

06 Remove the tray from the oven. The pastry should be dry and partially baked. Spoon in your balti.

07 Roll out the second layer of puff pastry and place it on top of the pie. Squeeze it along the pie edges. Brush the pie with egg yolk, sprinkle on some salt and then bake for 30 minutes until golden.

08 Cut up the pie and tuck in!

VEGAN BÁNH MÍ WITH MUSHROOM PÂTÉ [VG]

SERVES 4
1 hr 15 mins

Kornél Kovács
Pantalón

INGREDIENTS
walnuts
300-g (10½-oz) packet of
mushrooms
garlic
200-g (7-oz) bag of radishes
1 carrot
1 cucumber
white wine vinegar

01   Toast your walnuts in a frying pan (skillet). When done, set aside and clean out the pan with some paper towels.

02   Clean and finely chop your mushrooms and 4 garlic cloves.

03   Heat some olive oil in a frying pan (skillet). Add the mushrooms and garlic, season with salt and pepper, then sauté for about 10 minutes to evaporate all the moisture from the mushrooms.

04   Cool for a few minutes, and then blitz them in a blender with the walnuts until completely smooth. Leave to cool until the mixture reaches room temperature, then put it in the fridge until assembly time to let the garlickyness develop.

05   Thinly slice or peel your radishes, carrot and cucumber (de-seed these). Put half of this mixture into a jar with

granulated sugar
soy sauce
1 lime
extra firm tofu
baguette
fresh coriander (cilantro)
olive oil
salt and pepper

A VIETNAMESE CLASSIC, VEGGIE STYLE. PÂTÉ IS KEY TO CREATING AN AUTHENTIC BÁHN MÍ!

5 tablespoons white wine vinegar, 2 teaspoons of sugar and 2 teaspoons of salt. Make sure it covers all the veg. Chill for at least an hour. Set the other half of the veg aside.

06   Drain your tofu and slice thinly. Place on paper towels and pat dry.

07   To make the marinade, whisk together 2 tablespoons olive oil, 2 tablespoons soy sauce, the juice and zest of 1 lime, 1 clove of garlic and a good grind of pepper. Whack the tofu in a bowl and pour the marinade in. Make sure the tofu is coated before placing in the fridge for at least 15 minutes.

08   Add some oil to a pan and place the tofu slices in it, not touching each other. Fry for a few minutes on each side, until caramelized and golden brown.

09   Cut up a baguette into four pieces. Drain the pickled veg and chop up the coriander.

10   Cut open each baguette and layer on the mushroom pâté, tofu, pickled veg and normal veg, and top with some coriander!

SERVES 4

1 hr

Roy Ayers Ubiquity
Everybody Loves the Sunshine

INGREDIENTS

3 red (bell) peppers
whole milk
dried macaroni
paprika
plain (all-purpose) flour
Cheddar
manchego
olive oil
salt and pepper

**CHANGING THE MAC &
CHEESE GAME FOREVER.
MAKE SURE YOUR PEPPERS
ARE NICE AND CHARRED
FOR A NICE DEPTH OF
FLAVOUR IN YOUR MAC.**

ROASTED PEPPER MAC 'N' CHEESE WITH PAPRIKA & MANCHEGO

01 Preheat your oven to 180°C fan (200°C/400°F/Gas Mark 6).

02 Add your whole peppers to a roasting tray and cook for 45 minutes in the oven, until charred and soft.

03 Remove the peppers from the oven. Allow to cool. Peel off the skins and remove the seeds. Add two of the peppers to a blender together with a pint of milk and a good grinding of pepper. Blitz until smooth.

04 Get 500 g (1 lb 2 oz) macaroni on (cook for 10 minutes in salted boiling water).

05 Add 1 teaspoon of paprika and 2 tablespoons of plain flour to some olive oil and whisk it in. Start slowly adding the blended pepper mix, whisking as you do this. You should end up with a nice thick red sauce.

06 Add 300 g (3½ cups) grated Cheddar and 200 g (generous 2 cups) grated manchego. Mix it in until smooth.

07 Once the cheese is melted, add your macaroni. Stir it in. Slice up your remaining roasted pepper and add that too.

08 Stir everything together, and then top it with some more grated Cheddar and manchego. Whack the mac and cheese under the grill (broiler) for 10 minutes until golden and bubbling. Remove from the oven, spoon into bowls and enjoy!

INGREDIENTS

3 courgettes (zucchini)
1 red onion
2 (bell) peppers (not green)
1 cauliflower
400-g (14-oz) tin of chickpeas
cayenne pepper
garam masala
120-g (4-oz) pot of The
Coconut Collaborative Dairy-
Free Yogurt
fresh mint
1 lemon
1 cucumber
garlic
4 pittas
pomegranate seeds
olive oil
salt and pepper

SUCH A FRESH SUMMERY
DISH. THE POMEGRANATE
SEEDS AT THE END
PROVIDE THE PERFECT
COOLING BURSTS OF
FLAVOUR.

ROAST VEGETABLE GYROS WITH COCONUT YOGURT TZATZIKI [★] [VG]

01 Preheat your oven to 180°C fan (200°C/400°F/Gas Mark 6).

02 Finely chop 3 courgettes, 1 red onion and 2 peppers into bite-sized pieces. Break a cauliflower up into little florets. Place the vegetables into a baking tray. Pour in a tin of chickpeas, with some of the starchy water. Pour over a good glug of olive oil, add 2 heaped teaspoons cayenne pepper, 2 heaped teaspoons garam masala, a sprinkle of salt and pepper, and mix everything together. Place in the preheated oven for 30 minutes.

03 Tzatziki time. Pour a pot of coconut yogurt into the bowl. Add a small bunch of finely chopped mint, the juice of a lemon, and the grated cucumber. Grate in a clove of garlic, season well and mix it all together.

04 After 30 minutes, remove the roasted vegetables from the oven, mix them about, and then place back in the oven for 15 more minutes.

05 Assembly time. Warm 4 pittas. Load each with your spiced vegetables, then tzatziki, then some pomegranate seeds, then some more vegetables, more tzatziki, more pomegranate seeds, and TUCK IN!

INGREDIENTS (FOR BASE)

self-raising (self-rising) flour
natural yogurt
salt

RICOTTA, COURGETTE & FENNEL INGREDIENTS

ricotta
1 lemon
courgette (zucchini)
fennel
cherry tomatoes
chilli (hot red pepper) flakes
fresh basil
salt and black pepper

TALEGGIO, KALE & WILD MUSHROOMS INGREDIENTS

kale
wild mushrooms
garlic
fennel seeds
200-g (7-oz) block of taleggio
butter

CHERRY TOMATO CAPRESE INGREDIENTS

cherry tomatoes (yellow and red ideally)
garlic
buffalo mozzarella
fresh basil
olive oil

VEGGIE PIZZAS (3 WAYS)

01   Sift 400 g (3 cups) self-raising (self-rising) flour into a bowl. Add a very large pinch of salt. Add 300 g (10½ oz) yogurt bit by bit, mixing it through the flour with a fork. Keep adding it in and mixing it through until it is all in the bowl.

02   Flour a work surface and tip the dough out of the bowl. Flour your hands and knead – firstly lightly, and then build up the pressure. If it feels a bit wet, just add some more flour. Keep kneading until you have a nice smooth ball. Add it to a bowl and cover the bowl with a damp tea towel for an hour.

03   Preheat your oven to 200°C fan (220°C/425°F/Gas Mark 7).

04   Cut the dough into 4 balls and roll out on a floured surface. You want them thin. Add to a baking sheet lined with baking paper.

RICOTTA, COURGETTE & FENNEL

01   Add 250 g (9 oz) ricotta, the zest of a lemon, a very generous grinding of black pepper and a pinch of salt to a bowl. Mix well. Smooth the ricotta over the pizza base. Shave very thin slices of courgette and fennel over the base. Add a handful of halved cherry tomatoes. Sprinkle on some chilli flakes. Add some basil leaves, grate over a bit more lemon zest, season with salt, pepper and a very good drizzle of olive oil. Place the pizza in the preheated oven for 15 minutes until you have a crisp crust. Scatter some more basil over the top and enjoy.

TALEGGIO, KALE & WILD MUSHROOMS

01   Place some kale in a bowl and cover with boiling water. Break up your mushrooms. Add to a frying pan (skillet) with a crushed garlic clove and a teaspoon of fennel seeds. Add a knob (pat) of butter and fry the mushrooms down until they are caramelized and dehydrated. Top your pizza with fennel mushrooms, kale and slices of taleggio. Place in the preheated oven for 15 minutes until the taleggio is golden and bubbling.

CHERRY TOMATO CAPRESE

01   Add roughly 250 g (9 oz) of cherry tomatoes to a frying pan (skillet) with a glug of olive oil and a crushed garlic clove. Cook until the tomatoes are bursting and reduced down. Add the tomato sauce to the pizza base. Top with torn mozzarella and another 250 g (9 oz) of cherry tomatoes (halved). Tear over some basil, and place the pizza in the preheated oven for 15 minutes until crisp. Enjoy!

INDEX

THANK YOU

I would firstly like to thank the MOB team, Rupert, Felix, Sam and Joe. None of this would have been possible without you. Thank you also to Maddie for all of your help with the recipe development. You are a wonderful chef.

I would like to thank my mum and dad for their unwavering support, my brothers Joe and Sam for their constant help and advice, and all of my best friends who have been on call at all hours of the day since Mob Kitchen began. Misha, Tommy, Kit, Seb, Milo, Preston, Tom and everyone else. Thank you, thank you, thank you. Lastly, I want to thank my wonderful girlfriend Robyn. Your support is overwhelming, I love you.

Next up – MOB's brilliant design team, OMSE. James and Briton, thank you so much for your advice and help making the book look so beautiful!

In relation to MOB Veggie, I would like to thank my amazing photography team – Max and Liz Haaarala Hamilton on the camera, Charlie Phillips with the best props about and Alex Gray with the freshest food styling in town. I would like to thank everyone at Pavilion – Steph, Katie, Polly, Helen, Laura, David and Laura – for making this book happen, and my wonderful agent Cara Armstrong at HHB Agency for being my rock!